# "Soul & Spirit"

# "Soul & Spirit"

## Discovering Our Roots in Cape Verde

## Vasco R. A. Pires

Foreword by

Cher' no Salalhudin Omowali Mateus
Photographs by Vasco R. A. Pires

**To order additional copies of this book, contact:**
Xlibris Corporation
1-888-795-4274
www.Xlibris.com
Orders@Xlibris.com
58305

# Contents

Foreword ........................................................................9
Introduction ...................................................................11
Acknowledgments ...........................................................15

**Part One: Inspiration** .............................................. **17**
Golden Seeds ..................................................................17
Our Drum ......................................................................19
The Spirit of Cape Verde .................................................21
O Espírito de Cabo Verde ................................................23
Islands ...........................................................................25
People of Cape Verde ......................................................26
Gente de Cabo Verde .......................................................28
My People ......................................................................30
Nha Povu .......................................................................31
Fogo ..............................................................................32
Woman of Cape Verde .....................................................33
One of a Kind .................................................................34
Cape Verdean Man ..........................................................35
Cape Verdean Woman ......................................................36
Brava Girl ......................................................................37
Son of Cabo Verde ..........................................................38
Fidju di Kabu Verdi .........................................................38
Rain ...............................................................................39
Txuba .............................................................................39
Who We Are ...................................................................40
An Evening of Life ..........................................................41
Ernestina ........................................................................42
Lembrança ......................................................................44
Cranberry Pickers ...........................................................45
The Whaling Man ............................................................46
Looking for Azijah ...........................................................48
The Search ......................................................................49

Cape Verdean Mother ....................................................................50
Cape Verde, I Am Here! ...............................................................51

**Part Two: Roots** .....................................................................**53**
In Search of Our Roots ...............................................................55
Let's go to Cape Verde.................................................................58
My first trip to Cape Verde:.......................................................61
My second trip to Cape Verde: ...................................................63
My third trip to Cape Verde: ......................................................65
My fourth trip to Cape Verde:....................................................76

**Part Three: Jack Barboza** ....................................................**113**

**Part Four: ERNESTINA, the Spirit of Cabo Verde** .........**119**

**Part Five: Identity** ...............................................................**127**
I Know Who I Am, Do You?.......................................................129

**Appendix** .............................................................................**131**
The Republic of Cape Verde.......................................................131
Brief History of Cape Verde .......................................................135
SGI-USA....................................................................................137
List of Images—Credits..............................................................139
Bibliography...............................................................................141

# Dedication

To the memory of
Mr. Joaquino Barboza Brandu Fonseca
Born: October 12, 1901
Island of Fogo, Republic of Cabo Verde
Passed on: October 8, 2003
In Mashpee, Massachusetts, USA

\*   \*   \*

In memory of my grandparents:
For inspiring me to write this book.
Mr. Nicholau Rodrigues Pires
Ms. Rosa Pina Gonçalves Pires
Born on
The Island of Fogo, Cabo Verde

# Foreword

Vasco R. A. Pires is a unique Cape Verdean. He is a soft-spoken person with bright eyes, and a profound thinker. What makes him so special to me is, that he is a Buddhist, in addition, a Cape Verdean Buddhist as well! I never heard of such a combination, most Cape Verdeans are Christians, generally Roman Catholics. This man intrigued me. When he and I speak, he is always mindful of Cape Verde and humanism. He introduced me to Buddhist philosophy. He engaged my mind like no other man has done since Dr. Amilcar Cabral.

Vasco always spoke of the universality of humankind. The more I know of him, the more I see in his life, the spirit of Cabral. Vasco always said it is his "enlightenment." Cabral was a person of great enlightenment, which meant his "Buddha Nature."

When Vasco wrote his first book *"A Fraction of Me,"* his prose and poetry told the story of Cape Verde and his expressions of deep thoughts of the life of the Cape Verdean people. In the verse titled, "African Seeds," he makes the historical connection of Cape Verde with Africa. Vasco has ascended to the spirit of Dr. Amilcar Lopes Cabral (Abdel Djhassi). When he writes in our mother tongue *"Nu Bai, kel kabu ki nos kora san fika" (Let's go where our heart is.)*

Brother Vasco in his poems has the spirit and soul of the sweetness and beauty of Maya Angelo, with the strength, wisdom, and music of the great Cape Verdean Poet, Eugenio Tarvares. In Brother Vasco's sonnet "The Search," He refers to "AZIJAH" and asks how can I find Azijah? My grandparents from the island of Brava would use the term "Azijah" when speaking of Cape Verde in Kriolu; it was always "AZIJAH NOS TERRA" meaning Azijah our country. I ascertained years later when I studied with many Griots in West Africa that the word Azijah meant the mighty and the precious God. AZI comes from the Arabic root of Aziz meaning power and Jah means God.

We are returning to the source, and we have found our true voice. Azijah, Cape Verde the blooming Lotus Flower. Like the Native-American

Dream Catcher, Vasco has caught our dreams and vision, in our spirit and souls. Thank you Vasco R. A. Pires, I know that Amilcar Cabral is very proud of you, an African American-Cape Verdean de Azijah (Cape Verde), congratulations for "Soul & Spirit."

## Cher' no Salalhudin Omowali Mateus,

Lecturer and Consultant on Cape Verdean Culture, Fairhaven, USA.
*Mr. Mateus, an American born Cape Verdean, spent a period of his life before 1975, involved as an observer and communications assistant with Dr. Amilcar Cabral the leader of the **PAIGCV,** "Movement for Independence of Guinea-Bissau and Cabo Verde." In July of 2005 Mr. Mateus was awarded the Order of Amilcar Cabral Medal, by the President of Cape Verde, H.E. Pedro V. R. Pires, in recognition of his service to the Republic of Cape Verde.*

**(Fig: 1) Cape Verdean Heroes**

# Introduction

America is a land of immigrants. We each have a unique story to tell. Most stories will never be known beyond the first generation's memories. To fit in with the dominate culture; most immigrants were pressured into denying their cultural roots. They never passed on their language or cultural histories to the next generation.

Memories are treasures we enjoy in our golden years. We keep them alive by sharing with the next generation. My greatest treasure has been discovering the roots of my identity, my cultural base in the Nation of Cape Verde. This knowledge gives me pride; it adds unique perspective and value to my life. This book expresses my quest to discover my cultural roots.

My grandparents provided support for the first generation born in America to survive and strive for the American dream. They came to America to find a better life and future for those left behind.

In 1909 Nicholau and Rosa Pires, emigrated to the United States from the Island of Fogo, Cape Verde. They had four children born in America, Anna, Margaret, Roche, and my father Vasco. One daughter, Mimi, born in Cape Verde, remained there.

In 1947 at the age of six, my father brought me from Ohio to live with my Cape Verdean grandparents on Cape Cod. My grandfather was Portuguese educated and learned just enough English to get his U.S. citizenship in 1946. In his house only Kriolu (Cape-Verdean spoken language) was spoken. The neighborhood was primarily Cape Verdean and most was from the same area on the Island Fogo.

**(Fig: 2) Grandma Rose "Ke'Ke'"**

Sandwich Road, in the village of Teaticket, Massachusetts, was like a transplanted village from Cape Verde set in America. My grandmother, Rose "Ke'Ke'" was the friendly visitor of the community. She would walk the length of Sandwich Road (about two miles) at least once a week to visit relatives and friends, share the news, latest gossip from the Islands, and visit those who were ill. She would often take me along. The foundation of my love, pride, and longing to see Cape Verde was set. This experience became my wellspring of inspiration for my expressions of Cape Verde and the sea.

Religious belief has sustained me throughout my life. Cape Verdean people are traditionally Roman Catholic. In my early childhood, I was raised to be a Catholic. I was required to attend catechism to be indoctrinated into the Church. I received the sacrament of First Communion and then as a teenager, the sacrament of Confirmation. The Church served me well as a child, but as I grew more mature, the Church posed more questions then answers to life's meaning.

Religion to me is supposed to be a way to find answers to life's mysteries, and live a happy life as a human being. At age fifteen my search for the real meaning of God and religion began. My mother's side of the family was Christian. I then became a born-a-gain Christian till the age of 36. The Bible, I was told, was the word of God. God loved everyone. God knew everything and God was everywhere. God was so powerful, that nothing could stand up to him/her. My thought was, why then, is God limited to just one religious belief like, Christianity, Islam, or Judaism? Why does God allow so much suffering in the world?

In 1968 during a peace rally at Boston City hall a stranger gave me a newspaper called the "World Tribune." In it were articles about how people had changed their lives by saying the words, "Nam Myoho Renge Kyo." In it were ideas about creating peace in the world, one person at a time. I never saw that person again, but nine years later on Cape Cod, one of my students in my high school art class invited me to a Buddhist meeting. At that meeting, the "World Tribune" was being used to study Buddhism based on real experiences. They studied the history of Buddhism, and what it means to be a human being. After several months of checking out the people, the organization, and the history of Buddhism, I became convinced that this is what will give me the answers I have been seeking for the past twenty-two years. I have been a practicing Buddhist since 1978. (See notes: S.G.I.) During the past 32 years, I have learned to respect all people regardless of their belief. Most of all I have been able to respect and appreciate my own life and take full responsibility for creating value for myself and others. I have learned to understand the true power of religion and belief.

I no longer have to ponder the question of what or who "God" is. Having a respect for all life and its environment has given me the true meaning of "The Law of Life." A strong respect for self and others has given me a greater appreciation of our unique and diverse human family. To be proud of whom you are and whence you came is a gift that no one can bestow on you. To understand one's roots and culture is to validate your existence as a human being.

My most recent roots are on the Island of Fogo, in the young Republic of Cape Verde. Fogo is one of a group of islands in the archipelago called Cape Verde, located 455 Kilometers (less than 300 miles) off the West coast of Senegal, Africa.

In 1975, Amilcar Cabral led a struggle to gain freedom for the people of Cape Verde and Guinea-Bissau. After more than 500 years of colonial rule by Portugal, Cape Verdean people are free to determine their own destiny. Along with this new freedom came a renewed pride in what it means to be Cape Verdean.

Before 1975, religious authority, as well as the Government, suppressed African cultural expression on the islands as a way of controlling the inhabitants. Public expression of traditional music and dance, such as Batuku and Funana was not encouraged, because it was considered uncivilized by the Church and Government during the colonial period.

In 1995, these cultural traditions were the highlight of The Smithsonian Institution Folk Life Festival in Washington, DC. The festival was a celebration of twenty years of independence for this island nation. A pivotal event unified and promoted pride in Cape Verdean people all over the world.

This book is a tribute to Cape Verdean people throughout the world, who have kept our culture alive. Culture is what defines our unique human qualities and our values. It lives in our hearts, and in the core of our being, our souls. We have survived the harsh winter of colonial rule. Like "Golden Seeds," we have sprung forth into a new spring of independence. The heart is the most secure place to keep treasures that no amount of material wealth can buy and no one can take away. The Soul and Spirit of our Cape Verdean legacy is intact in our collective memories.

This book, **Soul &Spirit** is an expression, a validation, and respect for the contributions all people of African descent have made to humanity. It records my impressions of events, biographies, and observations that have shaped my outlook in life. It expresses my hope for the future. Its purpose is to impress on people of all ages and cultures, that each unique culture has value and is the prime source of our humanity.

—Vasco R. A. Pires

# Acknowledgments

I owe a debt of gratitude to my friends and colleagues whom have given me support in many ways in making "Soul & Spirit, Discovering Our Roots in Cape Verde," a reality.

First, my wife Clara Pires for her quiet support, love, and companionship. Next, my dear friends: Melanie and Al McNair, Caryl Hart, Barbara J. (Monteiro) Burgo, Ray Matthews, Jordine Roderick, and Sharon Duarte for their participation, inspiration and support. Mr. Marcel G. Balla, for his inspirational book "The Other Americans," continued inspiration and mentorship on the history of Cape Verde. Manuel Gonsalves, Cabo Verdean Creole Institute. Salah Mateus, (aka Cher' no Salalhudin Omowali Mateus) Cape Verdean hero who graciously contributed Foreword remarks to "Soul & Spirit."

Mr. Guenny K. Pires, Filmmaker and Dr. Terza Silva Lima-Neves, Professor of Political Science, for their assistance in English to Portuguese and Kriolu translations. Fred Marchant, Eva Bourke, and Keith & Heloise Wilson, and John Dean expert writers, who have given me, advise that continues to inspire me. To Jarita Davis for her inspirational chapbook, "There should be More Water." Karin Hines for her portrait photography used in the cover design. Candida Rose and Maria De Barros for their inspirational music getting me through the long hours of writing and rewriting of this book. To Daisaku Ikeda, my Mentor in life, President of Soka Gakkai International, through his poetry and actions for world peace, has inspired me share his struggle, to always fight on the side of justice and peace. My high school Art Teacher, Herbert Sunderman, who believed in me at a crucial time in my life, I am forever grateful. The president of the Republic of Cabo Verde, H.E., Pedro V. Pires for his vision and contributions in making Cape Verde what it is today. To Gunga Tavares, Attaché, Cape Verde Consulate, Boston for her help and assistance in travel preparations to Cape Verde. Special thanks to Cape Verde Airlines for four pleasurable trips to Cape Verde. To all my family and new friends in Cape Verde especially my cousin "Chico" and Antonia Pires, Manuel (Bo'Boi) and Lia Barros, and Mr. John Varela for hosting me in their homes while in Fogo and Brava. All the children of Cape Verde for their spirit of joy and freedom, they are the future of the Nation. Special thanks to Nuensa of Brava, (Fig: 7 Brava Girl). Takinha for kind hospitality of sharing her mountain home with us, (Figs: 4 & 23). To Leroy Gonsalves for his generous help and assistance during my stays on the Island of Fogo. To Moises Santiago of Brava, for his assistance during my four day stay on the island of Brava. To Nelson Rodrigues, Visual Artist, for an unforgettable trek up to the Volcano of Fogo. Madalena and Filomenha, Nelson's Mother-in law and Sister-in-law for their hospitality and the photo of Filomenha (Fig: 5 Cape Verdean Woman). All my new found Cape Verdean family and friends for making this journey to Cape Verde, the treasure of my life. Andy and Madalena De Andrade, founders of the Cabo Verde Children Project, for encouraging me to travel to Cape Verde and introducing me to travel within the country. Norberto Tavares, Rev. Imani Smith, and Jeanne Valles and the whole Cabo Verde Children Project team here and in Cape Verde, for making my first trip to Cape Verde a memorable one. Finally, Mr. Ray Almeida for his untiring activism in promoting Cape Verdean Culture.

Publications, where my work appears: "What is Poetry To Me?" National Library of Poetry's Anthology, Walk Through Paradise, 1995 and "I Can Swim in Your Eyes," Lyrical Heritage, 1996. "What is Poetry To Me?" Sound of Poetry, audiocassette album, 1995. "An Ode To MLK," N. L. P. Best Poems of The 90's 1996. International Library of Poetry's Anthology. "African Seeds," America at the Millennium, 2000. N. L. P. Editor's Choice Awards, 1995 and 1996. I. L. P. Editor's Choice Award, 2000. Works listed on The International Library of Poetry's Poetry.com, web site. "From Montgomery to Memphis," The Summer Review, Anthology edited by Jacqueline Loring, AuthorHouse 2002. "The Schooner Ernestina Family Ties," Mostra Catalogue, CV Expo 2008. Copies of "A Fraction of Me: Prose and Poetry for the New Century," AuthorHouse, 2003 is in the collection of the National Library of Cape Verde.

# Part One: Inspiration

I begin Part 1 of my story, titled Inspiration, with a poem inspired by the fact; Cape Verde was a base for the Atlantic Slave Trade. During this period, over 28,000 slaves departed for the Americas from the Cape Verde Islands. (Slavevoyages.org: the Transatlantic Slave Trade Data base)

The following poem is my expression based on the historical roots of my African descent. It is a poetic account of how we have overcome and risen above the negativity of our experiences in our journey to the Americas.

## Golden Seeds

Hundreds of years ago in the lush coastal forests and shores of West Africa, there were places where human treasures and culture abound. Evil beings, both black and white, lurked around.

They searched for human treasure to feed the greed of new world industries, Cotton, Tobacco, Sugarcane and Rum. Labor for free. Blue indigo Panu cloths, made by slaves in Cape Verde were used to pay the fee.

From West Africa to the Islands of Cape Verde, we were taken. Golden Seeds uprooted from paradise, to lands forsaken.

Family ties broken, brothers, sisters, sons, and daughters no more to be found.

Religious authority, strived to replace our spirituality. They tried to rob us of our humanity. Culture became our shield, protecting our hearts, minds, and souls.

To blood-red shores of the new world we are bound. Golden seeds carried by wind and sea. We sail to our destiny. We are taken from the "Green Islands" chained, in dark holds of ships, unwilling and prone. Our treasures of spirit and culture are all we own.

Golden Seeds bred in the hot beds of colonialism. Hybrid seeds of golden humanity set adrift on trade winds of slavery.

Golden seeds, tarnished by the rusting chain triangle, spanning the Atlantic, connecting the Americas, Europe, and the Caribbean.

In America, the Blue and Gray states engage in battle for high stakes. Blue prevails.

The chain is broken. Golden Seeds are free, free to bloom are we.

A new life we find, in our new country.

Before the sound of freedom leaves our lips, we are wished back to those dreaded ships.

Strangled by weeds of ignorance, hate, and bigotry we are stripped of our humanity. Again, we are denied, freedom of opportunity. Is America, a land of freedom, justice, and liberty?

There is peace and dignity for some, but not everyone. America, what have we done? Are we not equal? In truth, we are the same. Dignity and happiness we also claim.

We see other lands and cultures struggling for freedom and dignity in their homelands. All human beings are on common ground. We all have dreams and aspirations.

The Americas are now where Golden Seeds abound. Over four hundred years, struggling to reach the light, we now see golden seeds of hope, blossoming out the darkness. Will we continue to bloom, keeping hope, peace, and unity for all, in sight?

Yes, we can. Yes, we must. Yes, we will.

# Our Drum

Our drum was taken from us in recent history.
We thought it would never speak again.

Our drum sounds the word,
So our stories can be heard.

When we watch the nightly news on "TV"
The real world, we think we see, is not reality.

Education saved us from ourselves.
The truth has set us free.

Denial turned upside down,
We can now be . . . free.

Now, we have our sound, our cultural legacy
We can now reclaim our history hidden from us since antiquity.

We are free to pass on our legacy,
Free to let our energy flow,
Free to expand our life to its highest peak,
We can go wherever, we choose.
We can attain our goals.
With this drum, we can never lose.

The drum speaks.
We hear it loud & clear.
It sounds the call for all to hear.

Our true selves, of days gone by,
We can now finally see.
No longer must we live a lie.

Our drum is back, you see.
It speaks of our history,
Our ancestors left a legacy.

From the cradle of civilization this drum has come.
Returning to the source, our drum and we . . . are one.

# The Spirit of Cape Verde

Republic of Cape Verde,
Born in the midst of Atlantic waters blue.
Her children are one with the sea.

From all over the world,
We yearn to return anew,
To our, Island legacy.
Islands, once spurned, now revived.

Cape Verde, Cape Verde, we have returned.
Desires born of cultural pride,
Burning within our lives,
Wherever we may reside.

The sea surrounds us and unites us
With the universality of life's potential,
Always providing the essential.

The sea permeates our life
It sustains our communality.
With dignity and pride, we will abide

The tides of ignorance and false-history,
Of our cultural reality.
Who could deny the Truth,
Of our multicultural society?
Like the ocean, we touch all shores.

The culture of Cape Verde is like a hot bowl of soup.
Warming our souls; and lifting our spirits from the chill of wintertime.

Cape Verde, you should be proud,
Be strong, be the human paradigm.

Our spirit has unveiled the shroud
That has dimmed happiness in our time.

The soul and spirit of Cape Verde,
Is, what makes our lives so sublime.

# O Espírito de Cabo Verde

## (Portuguese translation)

Oh República de Cabo Verde
Nascida no meio das azuis aguas atlânticas
As suas crianças são unidas com o mar

De todo o mundo
Nós ansiamos o regresso Ao nosso legado ilhéu
Ilhas uma vez desprezadas, agora reanimadas
Cabo Verde, Cabo Verde, nós voltamos
Desejos nascidos de orgulho cultural
Ardendo nas nossas vida
Aonde for que possamos residir

O mar rodeia-nos e une-nos
Com a universalidade do potencial de vida
Sempre fornecendo o essencial

O mar permeia a nossa vida
Ele sustenta a nossa comunalidade
Com dignidade e orgulho nós vamos obedecer
As marés de ignorância e historia falsa,
Da nossa realidade cultural

Quem pode negar a verdade
Da nossa sociedade multicultural?
Como o oceano tocamos todas as costas

A cultura de Cabo Verde é como uma tigela de soupa quente
Ela aquece a nossa alma,
Ela moraliza os nossos espíritos do frio do Inverno

Cabo Verde deve ter orgulho
Sê forte, sê o paradigma humano

O nosso espírito desvendou a mortalha
E ofuscou a felicidade na nossa era

A alma é espírito de Cabo Verde
É o que faz as nossas vidas tão sublimes

# Islands

What is it about these Islands that attract me so?
I think of them wherever I go.

Like jewels in the middle of the sea,
Always beckoning to me.

Voices in the wind calling from across the sea,
Islands, calling from the past, reminding me,

Only treasures of the heart will last.

# People of Cape Verde

Cape Verde is a nation of people,
Forged on the "anvil" of colonialism.
It is a cultural bridge spanning the oceans of humanity.

Human waves, determined spirits,
Deep cultural roots, no one can deny.
To future generations, they provide pride and dignity.

A free nation, an example for all to see,
People of all colors
Creating this Cape Verdean democracy.

Pedro Pires, its president, carries on this legacy.
Amílcar Cabral, "Return to the Source," was his call.
Freedom and justice for all.

Cape Verdean people are proud, every man, woman and child.
Cape Verdean contributions made to the World,
Contributions, not yet recognized.

On the backs of Africans, many fortunes were made,
In that, "Golden triangular trade."
Sugarcane, Cotton, Cranberries and more,
Brought fortune and fame to this new shore.
America, her history, now revealed,
The truth, recorded, now sealed.

Freedom, justice, and equality, denied for many years,
Is now, a legacy earned by blood, sweat, and tears.
America, we have been here for many years.

We have toiled in the forests of the Americas,
The cane fields of the Caribbean,
The cotton fields and cranberry bogs of the U.S.A.

Whaling ships have carried our dreams,
Throughout the oceans of the world.
From far off islands and continents too,

We now unite to claim our due.
The power of electricity, combined with the new
Technology of wireless communications, and electronic mail,
The truth now spreads to the world.
The reality of the people of Cape Verde will prevail.

# Gente de Cabo Verde

## (Portuguese translation)

Cabo Verde é uma nação de gente,
Avançada "a bigorna" do colonialismo.
é uma ponte cultural que mede por palmos os oceanos da humanidade.

Ondas humanas, espíritos determinados,
Raízes profundamente culturais, ninguém pode negar.
As futuras gerações eles fornecem o orgulho e a dignidade.

Uma nação gratuita, um exemplo para todos verem,
Gente de todas as cores
Criando Cabo Verde democracia.

Pedro Pires, o seu presidente, segue este legado.
Amílcar Cabral, chamou-a "Voltam à Fonte."
"Liberdade e justiça para todos."
Gente de Cabo Verde é orgulhosa, cada homem, mulher e criança.
Contribuições dos Cabo Verdianos feitas ao Mundo,
Contribuições, ainda não reconheciliadas.

No dorso dos Africanos, muitas fortunas foram feitas,
Naquele comércio triângular de ouro.
Cana-de-açucar, algodão, morango e mais,
Fortuna e fama trazidas para esta nova costa.
A história da América revelou a agora,
A verdade, registrada e selada agora.

Liberdade, justiça e igualdade, negada durante muitos anos,
É agora, um legado ganho por sangue, suor e lágrimas.
América, estivemos aqui durante muitos anos.

Labutamos nas florestas das Américas,
Os campos de cana nas Caraíbas,
Os campos de algodão e do morango atolam-se em U.S.A.

Os barcos de baleia transportaram os nossos sonhos,
Em todas as partes dos oceanos do mundo.
De ilhas distantes e continentes também,
Agora unimo-nos para reclamar a nossa divida.
O poder de eletricidade, combinada com as novas
Tecnologias de comunicações sem fios e do correio electronico,
A verdade agora estendera para todo o mundo.
A realidade da gente de Cabo Verde, prevalecerá.

**(Fig: 3) Fogo Market Place**

# My People

My people, people of Cape Verde, people of the sea,
Islands of Cape Verde, portals to my history.

My people of the mountains surrounded by the sea.
The passion of the volcano,
My people, people of Cape Verde.

My people of Cape Verde,
Those people, of the nation, Cape Verde.
A people forever blessed.

Morabeza to all,
Whoever drops in, is always a guest.
My people of Cape Verde are the best.
Those people . . . my people.

# Nha Povu

## (Cape Verdean translation)

Nha povu, povu di Kabuverdi, povu di mar,
Ilhas di Kabuverdi, porta di nha historia.
Nha povu di montanhas, na meiu di mar.
Kel lumi di burkan,
Nha povu, povu di Kabuverdi.
Kes povu, di nasion Kabuverdi.
Kes povu, muitu bensuadu.

Morabeza pa nos tudu,
Kenhas vizita, nos un famila.
Nha povu di Kabuverdi, nôs o maior midjor.
Kes povu . . . nha povu.

**(Fig: 4) Takinha at Home**

# Fogo

See the island of Fogo, rising from the sea.
The black jewel of the Atlantic,
Fogo, island of regal majesty.

Fogo, crowned by Pico,
The black volcano, thrusting to the heavens.

Fogo, blackened by burnt offerings of
Liquid rock and ash from the core of Earth.
Spewing smoke and ash from its cone,
Pico has made its presence known.

The people of Fogo, tenaciously
Sustaining life on their island home.

Fogo, what do you mean to me?
You are the roots of my family history.
You have given me my love of the sea,

A reason to be.
Fogo, you are my eternal legacy.

# Woman of Cape Verde

Cape Verdean woman, with your talking eyes,
Telling stories of love, you hope to realize.
What man alive can you not hypnotize?

Cape Verdean woman, with your swinging hips,
Pano tied tightly around your waist.

Batuku, dance of rejuvenation,
Ensuring the survival of a nation.

Cape Verdean woman, with the power to beguile,
No man can resist your smile.

Cape Verdean woman, with your verbal quips
No man can resist your soft warm-butter lips.
Cape Verdean woman, so persistent and strong,
In your life a new nation you bear.

# One of a Kind

Women of Cape Verde, treasures from the sea.
Keepers of our destiny.
Through your eyes, we discern the times.
In them, a universe shines.
In your eyes, we can read our story.
It is a tale of hope, happiness, and glory.
Woman of Cape Verde you are one of a kind.

**(Fig: 5) Cape Verdean Woman**

# Cape Verdean Man

I am a man of Cape Verde,
Always doing the best I can.
I work with the land.
I am one with the sea.

I am a man of Cape Verde, you see.
I work with my hands as well as my mind.
I am a man of the finest kind.

Where ever I go people know
I am a Cape Verdean man.
I can be explosive as Pico and calm as the sea.

There is no man who can match me.
Uprooted from Africa,
Blended blood, from many lands.

A golden seed of humanity,
Tossed upon these once barren rocks, called Cape Verde.
I have survived and created, this unique island society.

I have sailed the oceans of the
    world.
Still, my heart longs to return
To the source of light for my soul
    and spirit,
Cape Verde, may this light forever
    burn.

I am a Cape Verdean man.
Try to understand me . . . if you
can?

**(Fig: 6) Fogo Man**

# Cape Verdean Woman

Cape Verdean woman, I see you in my dreams.
Your face, as bright and warm as the beaches of Maio.
Your passion, as hot and explosive as Pico, the volcano of Djarfogo.
You are, beautiful and mysterious like Djabraba.
You move, with the rhythms of Sao Tiago.
You are exciting, like the nightlife of Sao Vicente.
Boa Vista reflects in your eyes.
You are ageless, like the Dragoeiro tree, of Sao Nicolau.
Your body has the lushness of Santo Antao.
You, have the fragility of Santa Luzia.
Your smile, as bright and gleaming as Sal.
Cape Verdean woman, the world is in love with you.

# Brava Girl

I know a Brava Girl, with a mind so sharp and clear.
She cares so much for everyone,
All life she holds dear.

Often, you will hear her say . . .
Why do they treat people this way,
Far and wide across this land?

Her heart bleeds,
Watching man's inhumanity to man,
Woman to man, daughter and son.
Why can we not just live, as friends?

Before my life ends
I yearn to see us all living as one.
Brava Girl, do not give up.
There are many like you, who too possess
Life's, overflowing cup and share your point-of-view.

The circle is widening.
The causes we make today will endure.
The effects for tomorrow are secure.
Each day includes many more.
Brava Girl, the peace, you seek,
is, assured.

**(Fig: 7) Brava Girl**

# Son of Cabo Verde

The Son of Cape Verde is gone.
His life ended too early.
However, we need not be afraid.
For, his spirit, like the sea,
Is in all of us.

# Fidju di Kabu Verdi

(Cape Verdean translation)

Kel fidju di Kabuverdi dja bai,
Se vida kaba muitu se'du.
Kontudu, nu ka meste ten medu
Pa se spritu e mesmu mar
El na nos tudu.

# Rain

The rain! The rain!
The rain falls.
Cape Verde rises.

Rises, out of the sea
Of humanity's birth.
The rains may come, the rains may go.
The spirit of Kabuverdi
Will never die.

# Txuba

(Cape Verdean translation)

Kel Txuba! Kel Txuba!
Kel Txuba ta kai.
Kabuverdi ta labanta.

Ta sai di kel mar
De nasimentu di umanidadi.
Kel Txuba ta ben, kel Txuba ta bai.
Spritu di Kabuverdi
Ka ta mori.

# Who We Are

Cape Verdean woman, our destiny is set,
Our journey has begun.
We must show everyone
This struggle has been won.

Cape Verdean woman, work with this idea.
Reality is never what it seems.
Keep your mind clear.
Never relinquish your dreams.

Cape Verdean woman, we are on the right track.
We will never go back to that time of lack.
Unleash those forces within your soul,
Release them let them out!

Show the world,
What we are about.
Tell them please.
Help me make it clear.


We must show them who we are my dear.

# An Evening of Life

Music is everywhere.
The sound of a piano fills the air.
People here are free, to be themselves.
We are children of Earth,
Always happy and full of mirth.

We pause to stare, and compare,
Who is the most joyful of all.

I hear a haunting melody,
Supported by guitars, violins, drums and a horn.
Mingled with staccato rhythms, sounds of friends conversing
In heated dialogue.

Sounds that take me back to a place,
Where my "Kriolu" soul was born.
Couples dancing to fast-paced music,
Music full of life and energy, food for the spirit.

A Cape Verdean evening of life.

# Ernestina

Ernestina,
I sail on you at last!
Your history is part of my past.
You carried my ancestors across seas so vast.
Human cargo, carried from shore to shore.

In calm seas and storm after storm,
You carried them without harm.

Sailing, silently up Vineyard Sound,
Tarpaulin Cove lies off the port beam.
Music fills the scene.
People conversing, with sea chants filling, the air.

Moving along in winds so fair,
Wind filled sails to get us there.
Four sails drive you when the wind is blowing.
One iron jib keeps us going when the wind is slowing.

Ernestina, how graceful you are.
A lasting gift from a proud nation,
Cape Verde, you will always be,
My . . . inspiration.

(Fig: 8) Schooner Ernestina

# Lembrança

Remembering the traditions of the past,
We make the transition from darkness,
To enlightenment.

Transforming the reality of the present,
To hope for the future.

The future began in the jungles of Guinea-Bissau.
Brave men and women of African descent,
Risked and gave their lives for future generations.

Amilcar Cabral had a vision, a memory of freedoms past.
Hard work, sacrifice made Cape Verde free at last.

Generations born abroad,
Bring back memories of stories told about the old country.
Lembrança of grandparents, told and retold our story.

We make the connections from the past to the reality of now.
The task of reconnecting to our Soul & Spirit is now my vow.

# Cranberry Pickers

Little red berries, not round, but tart.
An American industry we helped to start.
On padded knees with scoops in hand
We picked the harvest of this wetland.

Men, women, and children too,
Made-up this cranberry picking crew.
Wages paid by the box or the hour,
We slowly develop our economic power.

In a few short weeks, it is all over.
Gone are the berries and all the green clover.
The fall season arrives in all its splendor.
Our money spent, on the food and clothes vendor.

Winter arrives the jobs are scarce or nonexistent.
With profits made from our persistence.
The bog owners are off to warmer climes,
While we survive on our nickels and dimes.

# The Whaling Man

I am a Cape Verdean Whaling Man.
I have seen many lives lost at sea
While I worked
In the whaling industry.

Families to feed and places to go
Adventure and a better life,
Were all good reasons for me
To venture out to sea.

I am a Cape Verdean Whaling Man.
To all corners of the world I have sailed.
Carried by trade winds,
I have followed the whales to far off lands.

Along this ocean highway,
Many of us would stray
From the ships to plant new seeds
In these exotic lands.

I am a Cape Verdean Whaling Man.
All four continents have been my hunting grounds.
Searching the bays and all the sounds, nothing was out of bounds.
For to catch a whale, was always in our plans.

I am a Cape Verdean Whaling Man.
From Brava and Fogo I have departed.
Around the world my life has expanded.
I now return to finish my life where I started.

I am a Cape Verdean Whaling Man.

(Fig: 9) The Port of Furna, Brava

# Looking for Azijah

Let me tell you a story of my search for Azijah.
Azijah is a place of mystery.
Our grandparents knew its history.

To us it is lost.
A part of our past, we must reclaim.
I will search to find Azijah again.

Azijah, Azijah, where have you gone?
I have looked in many places.
I have searched the World and the Universe too.

Azijah, you will shine your light, again.

# The Search

How can I find Azijah? First, I will ask my brother. *Brother, brother, where is Azijah?* My brother says, *I do not know go ask your sister.* I ask my sister. *Sister, sister, where is Azijah?* She says, *I do not know go ask father.* I asked my father. *Father, father, where is Azijah?* He replies, *I do not know go ask your Mother.* I ask my mother. *Mother, mother, where is Azijah? I do not know,* she said, *but you can go ask the sky.* Mothers are wise so I did as she instructed. I asked the sky, *sky, sky where is Azijah?* The sky answered, *Azijah is not here go and ask the mountain.* I went to the mountain and asked. *Mountain, mountain where is Azijah?* The mountain replied. *Azijah is not here. You must go ask the turtle.* I went to the turtle and asked. *Turtle, turtle where is Azijah?* The turtle said. *I do not know, ask your grandfather.* I went to my grandfather and asked him. *Grandfather, grandfather where is Azijah?* My grandfather replied. *Yes, I know where Azijah is, but you must find it for your self. Go and see your grandmother she will tell you how.* At last, I thought, grandmother will tell me where Azijah, can be found. Quickly I ran to my grandmother, sitting, down by the sea.

*Grandmother, grandmother where is Azijah?* I shouted. My grandmother looked me in the eye and said. *Ah, my son you finally realized what is missing in your life. You want to know where Azijah is. You must go to the shore when the waters are calm and still; there you will find Azijah reflected in the sea.* Always remember your heart, is the door to what you are looking for.

**(Fig: 10) Children of the sea**

# Cape Verdean Mother

A house full of children, all her own,
A Cape Verdean Mother is never alone.
She tends them all with great care.
Always, she has plenty of love to spare.

Always protective,
She shields them from harm or despair.
Cape Verdean Mother, mother to the world,
Treating all children as her own.

**(Fig: 11) Cape Verdean Mother**

# Cape Verde, I Am Here!

Cape Verde I am here!
A hazy predawn sky greets me.
A crescent moon shows me a welcoming smile.
Cape Verde, I have arrived!

Boeing 757 "EMIGRANTI" glides in, as smooth as a bird
On to the runway of my cultural past.
Home of my grandparents.
My cultural legacy, Cape Verde.

Just as I expected,
I find these beautiful and serene islands
In the middle of the vast West African sea.
Their voices, so clear, calling me to come near.

"Welcome, thank you for returning the spirits
Of your grandparents back to their beloved Djar Fogo."
"Djar Fogo" the ancient Island, the place of their birth.

Finally, I experience the mysterious black volcano "Pico,"
Sitting on Fogo like a crown. The fearless Soul & Spirit, of Txan.

(Figs: 12-13) Cape Verde We Are Here

# Part Two: Roots

(Roots) family, ethnic, or cultural origins, esp. as the reasons for one's long-standing emotional attachment to a place or community: it is always nice to return to my roots.—(New Oxford American Dictionary)

**(Fig: 14) Land of Our Roots**

# In Search of Our Roots

I am a second-generation American-born Cape Verdean. From the age of six, I lived in my grandparent's household. It was a home headed by my grandfather, Nho Nicholau Rodrigues Pires, son of Nho Domingo Rodrigues Pires and Anna Centeio of Fajazinha, Island of Fogo. In 1909 he and the daughter of Nho Manuel Pina and Margarita Gonsalves, my grandmother, Rosa Gonsalves Pina, of Largarice, Fogo, immigrated from the Portuguese controlled Cape Verde Islands, located 350 miles off the coast of Senegal, West Africa. They had one daughter, Mimi, who remained there. Between 1914 and 1918, two sons and two daughters were born. One of those sons was my father, Vasco R. Pires who was among the first generation of the Rodrigues Pires family, to be born in America.

In the years between 1931 to 1940, my father was one of many Cape Verdean men traveling to the American mid west, to find work in the steel mills and coal mines. My father finally settled in Canton, Ohio. There he meets and marries Mary Edith, an African-American woman from the hills of West Virginia. I was born one month before the attack on Pearl Harbor. America is at war. My father and his young family moved back to Massachusetts, he then enlisted in the U.S. Navy and was off to war in the Pacific. Some time between the end of the war and 1947, my parents divorced and I found myself separated from my sister, brother, and mother. I am left with my Cape Verdean grandparents.

This is the beginning of my Cape Verdean awaking. It starts with language and culture. My grandfather was granted his American citizenship in 1946. He was educated in Cape Verde, was fluent in Portuguese, and spoke some English. He earned a living as a landscape gardener.

My grandmother had no formal education, but was wise in life experience. She was a skilled farmer and hard worker. She grew strawberries and a variety of vegetables. In fall, she worked picking cranberries. Growing strawberries and her work picking cranberries, was how she contributed to the household income.

I learned many lessons about Cape Verdean culture from her. In our household and in the neighborhood, most adults spoke Kriolu. I quickly learned the language and the culture from the close Cape Verdean community of Sandwich Road, on Cape Cod, Massachusetts.

**(Fig: 15) Three Generations**

The families closest to us were, the Garcia family, Jenny and three beautiful daughters; Brenda, Donna, Rosalyn and 1 son; Frank Junior. Their father, Frank "Mane Santu," is famous for being the first man to have a successful cornea eye transplant. His story was featured in a national magazine. There was Isabelle a self-taught artist and her husband, Manuel "Prantxentxi" who was a vegetable vender, and community meat butcher. They also took in many foster children. The Andrade family of 20 children, whose mother Alice worked as a cook. The father, Manuel "Rapazin" was a carpenter and very knowledgeable self-taught medicinal herb expert.

My grandfather played the accordion and was always ready to play on festive occasions. Letters from the "Old Country" Cape Verde would tell of hardships being experienced by those unable to leave. "The Cape Verdean Club," formed in 1943, was responsible for collecting aid to assist them with clothing, foodstuff, and other essentials necessary for survival during the continuing drought and volcanic eruptions on the Island of Fogo.

I was exposed to the culture by attending the many festivals held during the year, honoring various saints of the Catholic Church. I learned to speak the Kriolu dialect of the Island of Fogo, while accompanying my grandmother on her frequent home visits. On some occasions, the Cape Verdean Club would show newsreels from Cape Verde, showing the conditions on the Islands.

My interest in learning more about Cape Verde came during my early teenage years. In the summer of 1956, the Schooner Ernestina arrived in Providence, Rhode Island. On board were family members from Cape

Verde. I was excited to be going aboard a real ocean going vessel that came from Cape Verde. I felt a direct connection with my roots, a spiritual connection that I am only now beginning to realize. I met my cousin Mane, my grandmother's nephew who was the ships' cook. Although I did not know it at the time, another cousin, Chico, my grandfather's nephew was also aboard as a passenger coming to America from Cape Verde.

Fifty-one years later in 2007, I find myself visiting with him in his home in Cape Verde. How mystical is that? Cape Verde is in my blood by birth. Over the years, it has entered my soul by association and my desire to make a direct connection with its spirit.

In 1975, after many years of armed struggle against the Colonial regime in Portugal, Cape Verde was free. Led by Amilcar Cabral, Cape Verde became an Independent Nation, the Republic of Cape Verde. I later learn that my grandfather's first cousin, Pedro Verona Rodrigues Pires became Cape Verde's first Prime Minister, and now (2009) the President of the Republic.

In 1979 in Fairhaven, Massachusetts, four American born Cape Verdean artists, Stephen Rose, Ben Barros, Maurice Costa, and I, along with Salah Mateus organized the first exhibition of Cape Verdean Art in America since the Independence of Cape Verde. The Fairhaven Universalist Church was the host for the event. The National Flag of the new Republic of Cape Verde was proudly raised and displayed for all to see.

On the twentieth anniversary of Cape Verdean independence, in July of 1995, the Smithsonian Institution in Washington, D.C. held a Folk-life Festival. The highlight of this Festival for me was the "Cape Verdean Connection." A comprehensive exhibit of Cape Verdean culture and arts. For many Americans, this was the first such view of Cape Verde after independence. For me, it was an inspiration to see and talk to Cape Verdean artists person to person, and in the language of our culture. This was the time I made my determination to travel to Cape Verde someday and personally discover my cultural roots.

I started working on several poems inspired by my desire to see the Cape Verde Islands. During this period of 1995 and 2002, I wrote and compiled several poems inspired by Cape Verde. These poems are included in a published collection of my first book of poetry titled, "A Fraction of Me: Prose and Poetry for the New Century," published in 2003. Some poems are reprinted or in revised form in this current work. This collection included several bilingual works written in English and Cape Verdean. Here is one of them:

# Let's go to Cape Verde

## (Nu Bai Kabuverdi)

Let's go,
Let's go where our heart lives.
Let's go to Cape Verde.
Jewels, in the middle of the sea.

Nu bai
Nu bai, donde ki nos korason sta moradu.
Nu bai Kabuverdi
Ko'nta na meiu du mar.

Let's go
Let's go where our heart lives.
Let's go to Cape Verde
Islands of destiny.
A culture, without mystery.

Nu bai
Nu bai, donde ki nos korason sta moradu.
Nu bai Kabuverdi
Isla di distinu
Un kultuda, ki ka ten nada gatxadu

Let's go
Let's go where our heart lives.
Let's go to Cape Verde
Where there is song and dance full of life
Swayed not, by war or hard work.

Nu bai
Nu bai, donde ki nos korason sta moradu.
Nu bai Kabuverdi
Donde sta kantiga ku badju intxidu di vida.
Nin Luta, Nin trabadju difisil, ta para nos.

Let's go
Let's go where our heart lives.
Let's go to Cabo Verde!

Nu bai
Nu bai, donde ki nos korason sta moradu.
Nu bai Kabuverdi!

This poem was my determination to encourage myself as well as others to go to Cape Verde and experience what it had to offer.

During this time, I was reintroduced to an old friend of my grandfather. Jack Barbosa, as he is known in America. Jack celebrated his one-hundredth birthday on October 12, 2001. I video taped this event and began a series of visitations to learn more about my grandfather.

Jack was excited to be able to talk to me in Kriolu. His mind was very sharp, and his memory was remarkable. He told me how he came to America from Cape Verde, in a two masted schooner in 1923 and how my grandfather had helped him when he first came to Cape Cod.

Over the next two years, I would visit with Jack and he would tell me his experiences and memories of Cape Verde. I asked him if I could tell his story. He said, "Yes, I want you to tell my story, you are family, I have long story."

How can I tell his story without going to Cape Verde? The question was how would I get there. On the same day as Jack's Birthday October 12, 1279, a Buddhist monk named Nichiren inscribed a scroll called a Gohonzon. It was meant to be a tool for the happiness of all humanity and the attainment of personal goals. With that spirit in mind, I was determined to somehow get to Cape Verde.

On October 8, 2003, just four days before Jack's one hundred and second birthday, he passed away.

(Fig: 16) Jack Barboza 101 years old

# My first trip to Cape Verde:

On October 12, 2004, on Jack's Birthday, I arrived in Cape Verde for the first time. I was part of a volunteer delegation to help establish a local presence of "Cabo Verde Children, Inc." a nonprofit organization helping to find sponsors for under privileged children in Cape Verde so they can afford to go to and stay in school. Among the delegation was, cofounder, Andy A., and delegates, Norberto T., Rev. Imani S., Jeanne V. and myself as the official videographer. We all agreed to pay our own expenses for this trip.

This first trip only lasted a week; I was able to visit the islands of Santiago and Sal. On Santiago, we visited schools and municipal leaders in Santa Cruz, Sao Miguel, Tarrafal, Osamada, and Praia. We were able to meet with the heads of State of Cape Verde, Prime Minister Jose M. Neves and the President, Pedro V. R. Pires. I did not know at the time, I was videotaping and meeting my grandfather's first cousin, the President of Cape Verde. He was my first contact with family in Cape Verde. Before we left Praia, I documented the official opening of the office of Cabo Verde Children project in Cape Verde. Our mission was complete and it was time for celebration.

In Praia, a party was given in our honor. Norberto Tavares, the honorary Ambassador for Cabo Verde Children project, and the Cape Verdean guitarist Bau, teamed up with other artists to perform for all the invited guests.

We say our goodbyes to Praia and depart for the Island of Sal and then home. We spent the last two days on the Island of Sal. For our last piece of business, we met with the municipal president of Sal to discuss the Cabo Verde Children project.

Andy rented a car and we drove to the resort village of Santa Maria to relax and take a tour of the Island. We visited the salt mine of Pedra de Lume and the lava tubes and natural swimming hole at Buracona. On our last night in Cape Verde, we dined at the Nha Terra Restaurant and enjoying the music of Ivo Nunes and the Mateus Band. It was a magical night in Cape Verde, the moon was full, the night was warm, and all was well with the world.

On this trip, I brought a photo of Jack Barboza with me. I placed it in the back of a framed picture in my hotel room in Santa Maria, Sal. At least

Jack's image is back in Cape Verde to celebrate his one hundred and third birthday.

As the plane lifted off from Sal, Cape Verde, I was already having feelings of "Sodade," a longing to return to Cape Verde. So it is, my first trip to Cape Verde as brief as it was, has changed my life forever. Experiences I will share with all. The videos, the photos, and stories heard will become part of the works I will create in the coming months and years.

I return home with mixed feelings, happy to have gone to Cape Verde, but sad that I did not have more time to spend there.

**(Fig: 17) Cidade Velha**

# My second trip to Cape Verde:

In February of 2005, I was again asked to travel to Cape Verde to assist with the Cabo Verde Children Project. We were on a very tight schedule, within two weeks time we had to visit many families on five islands.

First, the Island of Santiago, a brief trip to Fogo, visiting families in the villages of Igreja and Feijoal, and then we traveled to the Island of Brava.

We left Fogo and took a ferry to Brava. Arriving in the Port of Furna I thought of the old pictures I have seen of schooners laying at anchor in this harbor. It was hard for me to believe I was actually here. We stayed in Brava for four days visiting families and children in all parts of the island.

During our stay, we visited Vila Nova Sintra, Cova Joana, Nho Senhora Do Monte, Lima Doce, Cachaco, Santa Barbara, and Faja de Agua, the port where the famous schooner "Matilde" departed on it's ill fated voyage to America in August of 1943. Every day I enjoyed meals of fresh fish caught off the shores of Brava. I will never forget meeting the famous violinist Nho Raul, 102 years old he no longer played due to illness, he was now bed ridden, and near death. I am sure, during his lifetime, he created great joy with his music, for many people.

I was amazed at how beautiful both Fogo and Brava is, I had heard that they were dry and very poor. Everyone I met was like meeting a member of my family, always welcomed with a greeting and a smile. I have now experienced living in Brava and seeing first hand what it is, like to be a Cape Verdean resident. I felt like I was home. I would never again, feel like a tourist in Cape Verde. I would always feel at home here.

From Brava, we head back to Fogo to catch a flight to Praia. We had to sail back to Fogo on the Sloop "Senhora do Monte," captained by Jose Domingos Lopes. The ferry back to Fogo was delayed and would not get us to Fogo in time for our flight for Santiago. Captain Lopes was Brava's emergency transportation to Fogo. He built his 54-foot sloop over a period of twenty-four years in his back yard in Brockton, Massachusetts, and sailed it to Brava to retire. It was a proud moment and a dream come true for me to be sailing in Cape Verdean waters with Captain Jose Domingos Lopes.

After two days of home visits on Santiago, we fly to the Island of Sao Vicente. While in Sao Vicente, we traveled to the beautiful Baia do Gatos on the East side of the island. In route, we stopped to visit an orphanage to discuss collaboration with the Cabo Verde Children Project. We visited the famed From Sao Vicente we flew to Sal, where we spent time relaxing before our flight back home.

I have now traveled twice to the Republic of Cape Verde and still have not visited family on the Island of Fogo. I decided that I must return and spend an extended time on Fogo to get acquainted with my relatives there. I have spent a lot in cash and credit in my volunteer efforts to help the Cabo Verde Children's project, so I had no funds to go back anytime soon.

**(Fig: 18) Capt. Jose Domingos, Brava**

# My third trip to Cape Verde:

In June of 2005, Cabo Verde Airlines celebrated their fifty-year anniversary of air transportation in Cape Verde. They also became certified to fly their own planes between the United States and Cape Verde. A big gala event was held in Boston. I was asked to produce a video presentation to commemorate the event. The only stipulation was it had to be completed within two weeks. I gladly accepted the challenge and the loss of sleep it would require, during that period. This job became my ticket back to Cape Verde again. The presentation was successful, I got paid, and reservations were made for my return trip to Cape Verde.

In October of 2005, I was on my way to Cape Verde for two weeks. I planned to spend most of the time on Fogo to get acquainted with family there. To my surprise, my good friend Salah Mateus and his wife had also planned a trip to Cape Verde as well.

He was going to meet with the President of Cape Verde, the Prime Minister, and other friends he knew from the days before independence. Salah had received one of Cape Verde's highest honors, the medal of "The Order of Amilcar Cabral" for his role in the struggle for Cape Verde's independence from Portugal.

Before we even got on the plane, I found out, just how big my Cape Verdean family is. While sitting in the food court, I noticed a group at another table. I could tell right away that they were Cape Verdean. When they spoke, I knew they were from Fogo. Since they were more than likely going to where I was going, I decided to introduce myself, who my grandparents were and that I was going to find family on Fogo. It turned out that they were related to my grandfather. The woman was Antonia the spouse of my grandfather's nephew, Chico. Her son, my cousin Lucindo, insisted that we stay at their house while we were in Cape Verde. I was finding out, that not only was there family in Cape Verde I did not know, but family in the U.S. I did not know as well.

As the plane made the decent in to Amilcar Cabral International airport on the Island of Sal, Cape Verde, we were greeted by a beautiful sunny morning. The desert like landscape of the island seemed an unlikely paradise for many arriving here for the first time. To me it was like coming home. For Salah, it was a dream come true. He had played a role in the struggle for Cape Verdean independence, now he would see first hand, the fruits of his labor. When he got off of the plane, he knelt on the ground and kissed the independent soil of Cape Verde.

From Sal, Clara and I, along with my discovered Cape Verdean family boarded a domestic flight to the Island of Fogo. Salah and Nancy will be flying to the Island of St. Viceinte and then on to the Island of Santiago, we will meet back in Sal for our last two days in Cape Verde, before heading back home to the United States.

On the flight to Fogo, we pass by the islands of Boa Vista, Maio, and Santiago. We approach Fogo from the Northeast and fly by the majestic volcano of Pico. Fogo, rising over 6000 feet above sea level, impresses me; it is the highest point of land in Cape Verde. I am excited by the anticipation of being in the birthplace of my grandparents, who left 96 years ago, never to return. I feel so privileged to be the one, returning their spirits, back home.

Chico's son Nene picks us up at the airport. He will take us to the North side of Fogo to Mosterios. You can take from Sao Filipe to get to the North side of the island two routes: the northern route and the southern route.

**(Fig: 19) Village of Murro**

The main roads on Fogo are paved with pieces of rock laid together similar to cobble stones, but are not smooth. Sand is packed in to fill the spaces. It is a rough ride and hard on vehicles traveling over the surface. We take the northern route to Mosteiros. Along the way, it has many curves, dangers of rockslides and unguarded shear drops into deep gorges and the sea below. The road is narrow, and requires caution and courtesy (a toot of the horn) when approaching a blind curve. Traveling at night requires, nerve and good driving skills. The trip from Sao Filipe to Mosteiros takes about an hour or more. I still cannot believe that I am back in Cape Verde for the third time within the span of two years. In the next two weeks, I will walk on the same ground in which my grandparents lived and played as children. I will learn more about our family history and the Island of my Cape Verdean heritage.

**(Fig: 20) Traditional Stove**

We arrive in the village of Murro, Municipality of Mosteiros. Chico meets us at the door. He is so happy to see Antonia again. He welcomes Clara and I and tells us, there is no need to stay anywhere else but at his house, because we are family and will always have a place to stay when we visit Cape Verde. My cousin Lucindo takes us upstairs to our room.

Outside of the room is a large open deck with a view of the ocean. The ocean is our back yard. A ground floor courtyard is protected from the rocky seashore by a 12-foot wall, topped with imbedded shards of glass. Within this wall, a pigpen is located in one corner. On the other side is a shed housing a traditional African cooking stove is located. (See photo Fig. 20) We settle in and get acclimated to this tropical paradise.

It is October and the end of the rainy season. Everything is green; corn is growing in every conceivable spot of land. To the east of the house, the now abandoned Mosteiros airport can be seen, with it's black volcanic lava runway bound by the black lava rock coast, pounded constantly by the sea. In addition, it is bounded on the South, by cornfields and the mountain of Fogo. To the West toward the village of Fajazinha, I can see the Mosterios radio station perched precariously on the edge of a cliff overlooking the sea.

This will be our base for the next two weeks. I will try to meet as many relatives as I can and learn more about the Island of Fogo.

The first person I wanted to meet was my grandfather's youngest brother, Dje 'Dje. He lived just up the street past the Mosteiros, FM radio station, in a section called Fajazinha. He was born 13 years after my grandfather left Cape Verde. He and my grandfather never met. I brought pictures of my grandfather to give to him. At 83 years old, he was very fit and still actively working. I felt like my grandfather's spirit was overjoyed that I was able to connect with the brother he never met.

Before we left for Cape Verde, I was given a photograph of Anna, the mother of Charles (Marcelino) Monteiro. He wanted me to give the photo to his cousin Cosimedo. He said that Cosimedo lived near the airport. I assumed it was the airport in Sal. Therefore, I planned to look him up when we returned to Sal. Two days after arriving in Murro I was walking up the road from Murro to visit my cousin Nene, I stopped by a little store to say hello to some men sitting outside. I introduced myself, each of them the same. One man said, "My name is Cosimedo." I said, "Oh, you must be Marcelino Monteiro's cousin. I have a photo of your aunt Anna he sent you." I realized now, Marcelino referred to this airport. I ran back to the house and got the photo. (See image)

On this trip, I wanted to meet as many family members as possible. I also wanted to get acquainted with Fogo and the people who lived there. On my first brief visit to Fogo in February of 2005 with the Cabo Verde Children project, I met the president of the county of Mosterios, Dr. Fernandino Teixeira. Today, I was hoping to meet with him and learn a little more about Mosterios, the place where my grandfather and most of my relatives are from. He was gracious enough to take my spouse and I with him on a tour of the county to visit areas of interest and a school where he and his staff met with parents and teachers. There was also a presentation of books and school supplies to the school. I was very impressed with his respect and caring for the people, he served. He told me that, "Elected officials should serve the people and not exploit them." He took his job very seriously.

**(Fig: 21) Visual Artist, Nelson Rodrigues**

On a visit to the village of Igreja, I met a young man working on a sculpture in front of his house. His name was Nelson Rodrigues. I introduced myself, told him that I too am an artist, and liked what he was doing. It looked like he was carving faces into the sides of a drum. When I commented on the drum he was working on, he said. "This is not a drum, it is a very old Pilon." (A large narrow bowl used to grind grains) This Pilon was made of wood, and was almost as tall as his 5-year-old son, "Little Tony," who was standing close by watching hiss father work. What he was doing was transforming the Pilon from an old discarded relic, into a work of art with carved stylized faces around the sides.

We became quick friends. I shared with him my project of making a film about Cape Verde. He showed me a proposal for a project to form a visual arts co-op to give artist on Fogo and Brava a place to sell their art. I was very impressed with his vision and initiative. I offered to help in any way I could. Nelson supported himself and his young family by doing odd jobs like painting signs, fishing and taking people on tours up to the Volcano. I asked if he would take my spouse and I up there one day during our stay. He said he would make the arrangements.

He would pick us up early in the morning and take us up to the volcano. We would first hike up to Monte Velha Park. From there, we would catch a bus to Cha Das Caldeiras (also known as Txan) where we would stay over night at a small motel at the foot of the volcano, Pico. We would then climb to the rim of Pico in the Morning. That was the plan.

In coming to Fogo, I not only wanted to connect with family, but I wanted to connect with Cape Verde it self. I wanted to feel the soul of the country and the spirit of the people. Making this trek to the volcano was a spiritual quest, or "Tozan," (Japanese meaning to climb the mountain) to understand the heart of Fogo. I was not here as a tourist but here to discover a deeper part of myself.

On Wednesday of our last week on Fogo, before sunrise, Nelson arrived at my cousin's house to pick us up. It was before sunrise. We were driven to a location just beyond the village of Igreja. It was still very dark. We were let off at a side road in the middle of nowhere. Nelson led us to a small opening by the road. We will follow on our trek up to Monte Velha 6000.00 feet above sea level the footpath. We dressed light and we each had a small bottle of water. Nelson said it was a three-hour walk up to Monte Velha Park. From there, we will catch a bus that will take us to the volcano. No big deal, three-hour walk up the path, a bus ride, and we are there. I reminded Nelson that we are in our sixties and probably walk a little slower than most people whom have made this climb. He assured us that we would do fine. "We will take our time, there was no need to hurry," he said. "Just one step at a time and we will get there." He reassured us.

As we walked up the narrow path, we could still see the Moon, shinning it is last light, as the dawn slowly gave way to the Sun. The morning was still cool and comfortable as we made our way up the path. We passed many children walking, on their way to school.

Within an hour, it started to get lighter and our breaths got more frequent, the path seemed to get steeper. We left the footpath on to a narrow cobblestone road, cut into side of the mountain. Looking back toward the low land, as we climbed, the buildings were getting smaller, the sun was rising higher, and the temperature getting hotter.

At 07:30, an hour into our trek, we reached the village of Feijoal. We came across many children happily on their way to school. As we climbed higher, the mid morning sun was heating up. Already, I could feel a little strain in my legs and doubt started to creep in, as to weather, this hike was a good idea.

At 08:30, we finally came to the village of Pai Antonio. Well, it has been two hours, so it cannot be much further to the top. Here we rested and bought some bottled water. Outside of the store, we talked to a man and his daughter who asked if we would take their picture. I also took some pictures of a man and his burro, as well as the scenes of the village. At this point in our climb, we came across more vegetation and shade, which gave us protection from the heat of the sun. We asked Nelson if we were close to the top yet. He replied, "Don't worry about when to get there, just go one step at a time, and we will get there." As we continued our climb, we passed people on their way up and down, carrying bundles of wood, water jugs, and large containers of fruit and vegetables balanced on their heads.

Fogo seems to have three climatic conditions. First, around sea level, it is dryer and hotter. As we ascended, the vegetation became thicker and there was more moisture in the air. We were in a jungle like growth of broad leaf plants and patches of cultivated gardens. There was corn, oranges, bananas, and lemons. There were even coffee plants growing along the path. Then there is the area of the volcano, at 9,000 feet it must be very different, compared with our present location. We will see when we get there.

It was getting late in the morning and though the sun was hot, we were comfortable under the shade of the trees and vegetation. We took frequent rest stops; my legs were aching so bad I was not sure if we could continue. The reality was, there was no turning back. The higher we went the thinner the air, more frequent stops, and harder breaths.

At one rest stop, we noticed that we were above the clouds. What an amazing sight! Just above the cloud line, I could see what looked like an ancient stone house with a roof made of Palm leaves. Nelson informed me this was a typical house in this area. The walls were made of volcanic rocks found in the area. The volcano on Fogo is still active. The last eruption was in 1995. I hoped October 2005 was not going be the next event.

We pushed on. When we thought we could not move another step, we could see the roof of another stone house, perched on a ledge among the trees above us. Nelson said we would take a break there.

The house was just off to the side of the trail. As we approached the house, Nelson calls out, "Bon dia, Takinha, kumo nha sta?" A woman with a broad smile greeted us, she replied, "N sta bon, obrigarda. Nu sta tudu dretu?" She gave us a warm welcome and we all sat on lava stones in the shaded entrance of her house.

Takinha lives in the house with her daughter, Julia. She appears to be about eighty, but very fit. The house is built of lava stones and the roof is covered with palm leaves. The floor is made of flat stone tiles. Just out side the entrance, there are tools for gardening and a lava stone Pilon used for grinding corn. The view from the front of the house was spectacular. Looking down over the top of the cloudy mist, occasional breaks reveal the landscape and the sea below.

**(Fig: 22) View from Takinha's House**

Back inside the house, Takinha's daughter, Julia gave us each an orange and a banana. We were made to feel right at home. It reminded me of the times I went visiting with my grandmother, the host would always offer food or some kind of refreshment. I asked Takinha if I could film her and ask her some questions about what she thought of her life in Cape Verde. She replied with a smile, "Si." I asked her. "What do you think is the Soul & Spirit of Cape Verde?"

**(Fig: 23) Takinha at Home**

There was a long pause, and then a broad smile. I then said. "Your face tells it all, thank you." She then said. "I was born here and I will die here. I have everything I need." Her smile and beaming face was indeed the true spirit of Cape Verde.

After we had rested, we said our goodbyes and continued on our way. It was now about 11:30 as we made our way up. We continue to meet people with bundles of wood and bowls of fruit and vegetables balanced on their heads, on their way down to sell them in the villages below. At 13:30, we finally arrive at a group of houses at Monte Velha Park. Here we would catch a bus to Txan and the volcano. To our dismay, the bus has already left. We must continue our trek on foot.

The rest of the way to the area of the volcano was a cobble stone road. It was a winding hilly and exhausting walk with amazing views of the ocean and steep gorges and many varieties of plants. Some inclines were so steep; I wondered how any vehicle could make it up the incline. I was now thinking, I am glad we missed the bus. The ride would have given me a heart attack. There were many reports of buses going off the road and falling into the deep gorges.

As we walked, we could view glimpses of the volcano peak from time to time. At about 15:30 we arrived at a gatehouse. The men inside came out and said it would cost us a fee to be in the park. It was strange since we were leaving and this was the first time seeing any gate during our trip. Perhaps we bypassed it by taking the footpath instead of the road. We paid and continued.

The cobble stone road turns into a regular dirt road. We finally come to an open area covered with a large lava flow and a majestic view of Pico the most recent volcano on Fogo. It was like entering another world. To the right was a wall of stone rising up higher than the volcano of Pico. This wall was the part of the original volcano of Fogo. We were walking into the original crater, Cha das Caldeiras where the villages Portela and Bangaeira are located. We feel a great sense of accomplishment. Here the climate was more comfortable and not so hot.

The road, lined with tall trees, follows along the base of the cliff to our right; on the left is a broad expanse of rough rocky lava flows. The great black cone of Pico dominates the whole area. We meet several farmers on our way, "bon tardi," we say as we greet each of them.

We reach the first group of houses and are greeted by several little girls, whom spontaneously start singing a song for us. Even the children have a sense of the "Morabeza" spirit of Cape Verde.

We had a sense of pride and accomplishment for having climbed from Mosteiros all the way up here to the volcano. It took us almost ten hours, but it was worth the experience of getting close and personal with Fogo and the people. We were tired and exhausted, my legs were hurting, and every bone in my body was aching. We stayed overnight in the shadow of the volcano. In the morning, we watched the sun rise slowly from behind it.

We did not have the time or the energy to climb to the summit of Pico today, perhaps next time. We were content with what we had accomplished and the experience will always remain one of our fondest memories.

Saturday, we left Fogo to go to the Island of Sal. There we would meet our friends Salah and Nancy to spend a couple of days on the beach sharing memories of our trip to Cape Verde.

**(Fig: 24) Sal Beach**

# My fourth trip to Cape Verde:

In November 2007, I celebrated my sixty-sixth birthday. My gift to myself this year is a three-week stay in Cape Verde. I will spend the entire time on the island of Fogo, the birthplace of my fraternal grandparents. I have arranged to stay and visit with my grandfather's nephew, Chico. This will be my fourth trip to Cape Verde and my first stay of more than two weeks. I plan to meet as many relatives as I can and record images both photographic and on film. My grandfather and grandmother left Cape Verde in 1909, and never returned to Cape Verde. I am the first of the American born Pires family to make the trip and visit with family in Cape Verde, especially on the island of Fogo. The following is an account of my experience during those three weeks.

**10-30/10-31-07: Tuesday/Wednesday, travel days to Cape Verde.**
I leave Falmouth, Ma. at 14:35 on a bus to Boston and Logan airport. My journey of discovery begins.

Arrive at Logan at 16:30; check in at Cabo Verde Air Lines counter at 18:45, I check two bags to Praia. I chose to check them to Praia and recheck them to Fogo from Praia, (This way I am sure to keep control of my bags and avoid possible loss or delay of getting my bags in Fogo).

Passed through TSA security with no problems. The plane was scheduled to depart Boston at 23:10, but due to a delay in departure from Cape Verde it was rescheduled for 00:30 October 31.

While waiting, I met a man from Fogo, Manezin F. from the village of Cova Figueira. He worked many years in the U.S. and is now retired. He spends his winters in Fogo and returns to Boston in the summer. Manezin tells me that he came to America at the age of 14 in the year 1946.

At 00:05 we boarded the plane. At 00:25 we depart the gate and taxi to the runway. In no time, the plane was at the runway and immediately takes off. As we ascended into the night I was able to get some video footage of the lights of Boston slowly fading into the darkness as we winged our way toward Cape Verde, six and half hours away. The Captain estimated six hours and 15 minutes flight time to Praia.

At 02:30, we were served our first meal. At 03:00 I could see the Big Dipper constellation just forward of the left wing at about 30 degrees altitude. The sky was clear with bright stars above, clouds, and haze below.

The plane cruised along smoothly as we had our dinner of chicken with noodles, corn and a fresh garden salad with crackers. This was all topped off with red wine, desert, cheese, and tea. We cruise smoothly into the night on course to Cape Verde.

Dawn approaches. I can see the Big Dipper at about 70 degrees altitude. At about 05:00 I can see a glimpse of the sun rising. Below us is the sea, with luminous patchy clouds between. The sky is becoming a beautiful blue as the sun slowly rises brightly above the horizon at about 15 degrees. 08:30 CV time we are served breakfast, a ham, and cheese sandwich, strawberry yogurt, a cookie, and coffee. We arrived in the Praia area at 09:30 CV time. Six hours after leaving Boston. We landed at 10:00 at Praia International Airport.

At 10:10 going through customs, I had a little delay. I did not have a visa. The Boston Consulate office said I did not need one. I was asked to step aside. I then spoke to a supervisor and showed him my documents of family relationships in Cape Verde and application for duel citizenship. He then instructed the security officer to allow me to pass through. Whew! I was afraid I would be sent home and not allowed to enter Cape Verde.

The flight to Fogo was due to depart at 11:00 so there was not much time to claim my baggage and check in for the flight to Fogo. I picked up a baggage cart (which is free in CV) and went to the baggage claim area.

One bag came through the conveyer right away, but the other one was taking longer. I started to panic a little because bags have been known to disappear and all of my chargers for my cameras and computer were in that bag. At about 10:40 the bag finally came through, now I wondered if I had time to get to the domestic flight check in station on the other end of the terminal and get the bags checked on the flight to Fogo.

I did not have time to get a phone card or exchange dollars to CVE (escudos). As it turned out the departure time to Fogo was moved up. I got checked in, got my boarding pass, and headed back to the other end of the terminal to the domestic departure gate. Outside I could see the planes lined up on the tarmac. Cape Verde Airlines had just bought two new French made planes, ATR, 72-500s, that carried 68 passengers each.

At 11:15, we board and at 11:30, we take off for Sao Filipe. The plane is very comfortable and the Cape Verdean pilots are very skilled. Several of them are graduates of Bridge Water College with two being women.

The flight was smooth and took about 20 minutes. I was seated beside the Commandant of Police in Sao Filipe, Dinato F. I was seated in the isle seat and just aft of the props, so I had to shoot video across Dinato's seat.

There was an empty seat up forward of the prop, so when the plane reached cruising altitude and the seat belt lights were off, I moved to get a better shot of Fogo and the landing into Sao Filipe. The view was amazing. The landing was very smooth, the plane used up every bit of available runway. The new ATRs require a little longer runway than the old smaller ATRs. I understand that there are plans to extend the runways at Sao Filipe. At this time, only the skill of the pilot makes it possible to safely take off and land here. In Cape Verde, you make the best of all situations. Cape Verdean people are among the most resourceful in the world.

We arrived safely in Sao Filipe about 12:00. Leroy G. and "Bo 'Boi'" (Tony de B.) were there, waiting for me at the airport. Our first stop was to get some money exchanged, as I had no Cape Verdean cash on me. For $120.00 USD, I got about $10.000.00 CVE. Leroy refused to take any money for gas and gas was about $7.00 USD per gallon for regular. After getting gas, we headed for Mosteiros.

I could not believe I was back on Fogo and in Cape Verde for the first time on my own! I will be here for three weeks, plenty of time to get acquainted with Fogo, as well as meet and visit with as many of my relatives as possible. Leroy drives the northern route to Mosteiros. This winding cobblestone highway connects Sao Filipe with the northern part of Fogo.

**(Fig: 25) Cousin Chico**

We arrive in the village of Murro (a part of Mosteiros) at about 15:30. I will be staying with my cousin "Chico," my grandfather's nephew. Chico's house is built like a small rooming house. It is located on the edge of the ocean, and consists of three single bedrooms, and two suites. They are all located on the second floor of the house. The first floor has an inner courtyard with a kitchen and utility rooms on both sides. Out back on the seaward side is a walled work area for chickens and a separated pigpen. A traditional cooking area is located in an open shed on the backside of the house. The front side of the house is where the living room, a sitting room, and two bedrooms are located.

I entered the house and "Chico" is waiting for me. He tells me what room to take upstairs. I introduced him to Leroy and Bo 'Boi. After putting my bags in my room, I asked Leroy to take me into Igreja to get a supply of bottled water. I buy two large 2.5-liter jugs. We return to Chico's, sit, and talk. Chico comments he has not been feeling well. He has been constipated and not getting around very well.

Leroy and Bo'Boi leave and I sit with Chico for a bit. I showed him pictures that I took of him and the family on my last trip to Cape Verde in 2005.

At about 17:00 I went up the street to see Tony and Katrina, stopped by Quito's to deliver pictures of him and his brother from 2005. Tony and Katrina are getting ready to leave for the U.S. on Friday. We had coffee and crackers. I wished them a safe trip and went back to Chico's.

On the way back to Chico's I saw Cristiano A. and Alerio P. We talked briefly and we agreed to talk later.

Chico and I sat in the kitchen and talked for a while. He asked me how old I was. "Kantu anu ki bu ten?" He asked. I will be 66 on 3 November. "Mi ten sesanta ses anu na tres di Novembre." I replied. He said he was 77 years old, just 10 years older than me. He said he would be happy when Antonia returns home from America on November 9.

At about 19:30 Chico went to bed. It has been a long two days of travel for me and I was ready to get some rest and plan for the weeks ahead. I recited gongyo, (Buddhist prayers) and went to bed. It is difficult to describe the feelings I am having now, being back in Cape Verde for the fourth time in three years.

With the constant sound of the sea crashing into the shore, I drift off to sleep.

**11-01-07 Thursday:** Today is a holiday in Cape Verde. At 0:500, I am out of bed, wash, and recite gongyo. I then go down stairs and check on Chico. He said he had a fever last night. Chico's daughter, Natalia came and made us breakfast, coffee and fresh bread. Chico had milk and "Kamaka." (A finely ground, baked corn flour) Around 08:00 two of the village children, Cristiano and Henrique came to visit. I showed them the photo I took in 2005 of two boys on a burro. They identified them as John and Wilson.

Later I went up to visit with my cousin Nene and Meme who live in the village of Sumbango. I gave them a Red Sox outfit as a gift for the baby, 1-year-old Diogo, and express my condolences for the loss of Diogo's twin who passed away last spring. Diogo is a lively baby boy, getting into everything. He is very curious about his new world. Had breakfast with them. After breakfast, my cousin Tata gave me a ride into the village of Qaimada-Guincho to make a phone call at the public phone. I called my wife Clara to let her know that I had arrived OK. (Cost 240.00 CVEs for about 3 minutes.) On the way back to Chico's, I stopped back in Sumbango to see Cosimedo. I gave him regards from his cousin in the U. S., Tony M. "The Colonel." In 2005, I delivered a picture of his Aunt to him. It was a gift from "The Colonel."

I returned to Chico's about 14:00, Natalia had made Lunch for us. After lunch I finished cutting and sorting the photos from 2005. Gave Chico pictures of himself, Natalia, Antonia, and cousin "Moodu." I then went up to my room to setup cameras, charge batteries, plan for home visits, and recording my visit on video and photos.

At 17:50, I sat outside with Chico. He summoned one of the local kids, and asked him to go up the street to Coleto's to get me a beer. (Cerviega) "Super Bock" he said, as he gave the kid $100 CVEs coin to buy it. When the boy came back, I gave him a bag of "M&Ms." Chico has diabetes, so he did not have a beer at this time. At 18:20, the streetlights came on.

At about 19:00, we ate supper. It consisted of beans, rice, manioc, bread, and water. At about 19:45, Chico went to bed. At 20:00, I went to my room, recited gongyo and read Jarita's book, "There Should be More Water," a book of verse on her impressions of Cape Verde. While reading I was listening to the song, "Kabu Verdi, Un Dia" by Candida Rose on my mp3 player. I was very inspired and could not hold back the feelings that came upon me at this moment. I had to cry. It was an extra special feeling of being in Cape Verde and on the Island of my heritage, in the house of my grandfather's nephew, Chico.

**11-02-07 Friday:**

At 0:500, I was awake. The sound of the breaking waves in the back of the house are relentless, as the tide gets higher, the sound gets louder. This sequence repeats all night. I think to myself. "Relentless is the sea/It is not like you and me/We stop at obstacles/We try to figure a way around it or to overcome/The sea is relentless/It never stops to figure a way around/But continues relentlessly toward its destination."

At 0:600 I get up, go to the bathroom, wash up, brush my teeth, making sure I use the bottled water, not tap water to rinse. The morning is cool, and the sound of the sea continues.

At 06:45, I do gongyo, about 07:15 go down stairs, and join Chico out side taking in the morning air and greeting people as they begin their daily routines. We wait for Natalia.

**(Fig: 26) Cousin Natalia**

At 07:45, she arrives to prepare breakfast for us. She carries a large basket of corn and beans on her head. (See picture) Today's breakfast is fresh-ground Fogo coffee, grown in Chico's coffee fields, fresh bread with two fried eggs, a special treat today! She pours coffee for Chico. Chico and I enjoy our breakfast. I thank Natalia for making us breakfast. She nods, smiles and says she will be back later to prepare lunch.

09:00, I went for a walk to the village of Igreja. On the way, I stopped by Cosimedo's to drop off more photos. I stopped in the village of Sumbango to see construction going on at my cousin Tata's new house and auto repair garage. Another cousin, Nicholau is building a house on the corner. I continue walking down past Chico's cornfields, meeting Natalia on the way. She had been out working in the fields and was on her way to feed Chico's cows.

At 10:00, I stopped by the Mosterios cemetery. Today is a day to visit the dead. Many people were gathered and a priest was saying a special Mass. I looked around at headstones to see if there were any names of relatives. I found at least three that appeared to be. I made offerings of water and diamoku (chanting Nam Myoho Renge Kyo) for each of them. (Note: Little did I know, at the time, that in two weeks time my cousin Chico would be buried here)

At 10:30, I continued on to Igreja. As I walked along the sea wall, I observe many names scratched into the top of the concrete cap. One name caught my attention, as it was the name "Djiny." Jarita Davis mentions the name in her book, "There Should be More Water." "Could this be the same person from Brava she mentioned sharing mangos with?" I wondered.

At 11:37, I arrived in Igreja. I stopped in to see the pastor of a church, Manuel, and his wife Julinda. I told him that I was assisting the Director of the Cabo Verde Children's Project. I needed to verify information on Elisa, a 7-year-old child on Fogo being sponsored by my cousin John in America. The pastor showed me the records of Elisa who receives the money that her sponsor, John, had sent. The parents have to sign and verify that the child is in school and doing well. This church in Fogo has volunteered to receive funds for distribution to all sponsored "CVC Children" of Fogo. I am hoping to get to visit her while I am here and give her a gift from my cousin John.

At 12:00, I visited with "Tony" Nelson Rodrigues, his wife Filomena and their son, little Tony, Jr. They were very happy to see me. Little Tony had grown a lot since I saw him last in 2005. Nelson invited me to go fishing with him on Friday.

Returned to Murro and stopped by to see Cosimedo. There I met another cousin Miguel. He is in his twenties, was born in America, and spoke English. He works in a store where he makes $120.00 a month. He told me he came to Fogo to make a new start. "Things were not going well for me in America," he said.

Tomorrow is my birthday and I had hoped to be able to go up to the Volcano, but it will not be possible without proper planning. Therefore, I will take a trip around the island to get to know Fogo a little better. I will take a Lugar (bus) to Sao Philip in the morning. I happened to see the driver Agusto at Cosimedo's. He said to be out in front of Chico's at 06:00 and he will pick me up.

**11-03-07 Saturday: HAPPY BIRTHDAY VASCO!** At 05:00, I wake up; wash, do gongyo, and get ready for my great day, on the Island of Fogo.

At 05:45 Chico was up and waiting for me at the front door. The Lugar (bus) came promptly at 06:00. As I was boarding, Chico seemed to be upset and told me, "You have plenty of family in Sao Filipe that you can stay with, why don't you take all your bags and go there." I could not believe he was serious, I thought he was just joking. As I boarded the bus, I had mixed feelings about the day, my sixty-sixth birthday on Fogo, the Island of my grandparent's birth, and how I am spending the day learning more about my roots. I thought about Chico and what he said to me. (Note: I later realized that he told me earlier in the week, that there would be a Mass for his sister Shauna today, but I had no idea it was more than just a mass at the church. I was ignorant of the fact that today was the thirtieth day after his sister Shauna's passing and this day was a special mourning day for family and friends. That is why he was angry with me for not respecting this day.)

Agusto, the bus driver made his rounds down to the end of Fajazinha, picking up passengers as he continued back through Murro and Sumbango. He then moved on to Igreja, picking up passengers and packages to deliver along the route to Sao Filipe. We took the southern route, which passes through the villages of Corvo, Ached Grande, Relva, Cova Figure, Salta, and ending up in Sao Filipe. This route gives you great views of Pico and the beautiful sunrise over the ocean. The road is very narrow and curves are sharp with very steep drops leaving very little margin for error by the driver.

The road is made up of closely fitted stones and the ride is not smooth. The bus is not in the best of shape. It seems that it will fall apart at anytime during the trip. If it has shock absorbers, it is not evident.

It is the end of the rainy season and vegetation is still green. The last growth of corn can be seen everywhere in any patch of soil it can possibly be planted. At this time of the morning, you come across men and women going to work or some just sitting out taking in the morning sun. I see groups of children with little backpacks walking on their way to school.

I arrived in Sao Filipe around 08:00 and walked down to the Seafood Restaurant located just south of the main church of Sao Filipe. There I had breakfast and called Leroy G. at about 09:20. He will be coming to meet me and show me around the city.

While waiting for Leroy, I spoke to one of the Lugar drivers. I asked him if he knew my cousin Emma who lived in Largarice. She was the daughter of my aunt Mimi. He was from that area and knew the family. He said she lived with her son Salvador. "Just ask anyone for Salvador and they will direct you to his house," he said. Leroy and "Bo boi" arrived at about 10:15 they joined me for breakfast. I used the public telephone to call Clara at home. (Note: the public phone was a regular phone hooked up to a box that kept track of the connection time.) The phone call to the states, breakfast for the three of us, cost $2,145.00 CVE (About $15.00). After breakfast, we went back to Leroy's apartment. Leroy showed me where my cousin Louis, the head of the schools in Sao Filipe, lived. I was hoping to meet him while I was there. He is also running to be elected mayor of the Municipality of Sao Filipe. He was not at home, so I was not able to meet him that day.

The Lugar (bus) to Murro was due to leave at noon, so Leroy took me back to where the bus departs. We made a short visit to the outdoor market nearby. I took some pictures and then got on the bus to return to Murro. The bus again took the southern route back to Mosteiros.

With today's trip, I have been completely around Fogo by having traveled both the Northern route and the Southern route. I have been up to the Volcano; I have walked up to the highest area and the lowest area of Fogo. I have done what many who were born here have not done. If only my grandparents could have been alive to witness it. I know they would have been proud of me. When I returned to Chico's I apologized to him for not realizing or understanding the importance of what today was to him and the family. He seemed to understand, as he did not ask me to leave.

**11-04-07 Sunday:** 06:00 I am out of bed, recite morning prayers. After prayer, I go down and sit outside with Chico. At about 07:00 Natalia arrived to prepare breakfast. After breakfast, Chico and I went for a walk.

He showed me the extent of all the land he owned, which was filled with an ocean of green corn growing on every available tract. He showed me the large tract of land he owned that is going to be a new hospital for Mosteiros. As we walked, I took many pictures of him and his cornfields. We walked past my cousin Nato's new house, now under construction. We finally stopped to rest at Anna and Jose's house. Anna came out and offered us a seat in the shade of the house. Chico sent one of the local kids down to the store to get us a beer. We sat across the road in the lot where the hospital was being constructed; there was a goat with its two kids playing. Chico asked me to videotape them. I did so. I also was told that Anna's family name is Galvao and she is related to me by way of (Joszinho di Pa' Pa'), a relative of my grandfather. After resting awhile, we finished our beer and started our walk back to Murro.

**11-05-07 Monday:** 06:00 up, washed, did gongyo, and went down to sit with Chico. At about 07:00 Natalia arrived to prepare breakfast.

(Fig: 27) Cousin Chico and Grandson, Diogo

After breakfast, Chico and I went for a walk. We went to see his son Tata's house and auto repair shop under construction. His son Nicolau also had a house under construction. We met Nene and his year old son Diogo in front of the house that Chico's son Lucindo had started construction on. I took pictures and video of Chico holding Diogo and pictures of Chico's cows and young pigs. Natalia and two boys were in the fields working.

My cousin Viriato arrived and asked me to come with him to see his grandmother, my cousin "Te'Te,"and meet other relatives in Fajazinha. We also stopped by to see my grand uncle "Dje'Dje,"and his wife Maria. I gave them copies of photos I took of them in 2005. We left "Dje'Dje,"and Maria and continued down toward the bay. I took pictures of the bay and the surrounding area where grandpa grew up as a child. There were people working on building a sea wall for the road extension leading to the bay and the fishing boat landing. I stopped to take photos.

There was much construction activity on infrastructure. I noticed many new gas meters being installed on houses. The roadway was being widened and resurfaced with new stones. There were many new houses being built and older homes being repaired.

We continued on to an area called the canal. I believe they were in the process of building a reservoir for water that would be pumped from the well that was hooked up to the village water distribution system. There I saw my cousin Natailio and other men working in the rock quarry. I took video and stills of the activity. Natailio was one of many Cape Verdean young men returning to Cape Verde after living in the U. S. as a teenager. I was Natailio's Art teacher when he attended High School in America. He works hard to support his family and runs his own barbershop. This afternoon Viriato and I will go to his shop to get our hair cut.

While at the barbershop we discussed issues facing Cape Verde. There is plenty of work that needs to be done. The biggest problem is wages. Those that do work, make only enough to get by. In some cases, the payment is literally in food. Presently there is no minimum wage. Natailio says that he could get by on what he makes in his barbershop, but he prefers to work at other jobs to supplement his income. He also told me that the men he was working with in the quarry, asked him, "Who was that tourist [referring to me] taking pictures?" He told them that I was not a tourist, and I loved Cape Verde more than they did. He told them that I was in Cape Verde connecting with family.

**11-06-07 Tuesday:** Up at 06:00 washed and did Gongyo. At 0645 Chico was getting up. At 07:00, Natalia arrived to make breakfast. After breakfast, Chico and I went for our morning walk. We stopped at Cosimedo's. Viriato was supposed to meet me at 09:00 to go up the strada (the road going up the mountain), and walk over above Fajazinha and down the old road to the fish landing near the bay. He did not show up. I decided to walk over to Igreja to buy two large gallon jugs of water and make another tour of Igreja. I stopped at the BCA bank and exchanged $200.00 usd for +/-$14,000.00 CV escudos; $1,000.00 CV was deducted for Bank commission and tax. I continued up to the village center and went over to the beach where the artist Tony had his studio and gallery. I took off my shoes and went out to walk on the black sandy beach. I took several pictures and video of some children who sang a song for me.

On my way back to Murro I bought two jugs of water and using some nylon cord I bought at a Chinese variety store, I tied the two jugs together and slung them over my shoulder. They were very heavy and I had a long walk ahead of me under a hot sun. This experience showed me what people here have to go through every day because they cannot afford a taxi or a bus. I met a high school teacher along the way, his name was Luis S., and he taught at the high school. I told him that I was a retired high school teacher and would be interested in visiting his school before I left. We agreed to meet later in the week.

**11-07-07 Wednesday:** Up at 06:00, washed, did gongyo. Today I have an appointment to meet with the President of Mosteiros, Fernandino at 08:00. I left Chico's at about 07:10 and arrived in Igreja about 07:50. I got to meet with the President at 08:45. I gave him some pictures I took of him in 2005 when he took Clara and me with him on his visit to a school to present books and supplies. Moreover, I gave him a copy of the photo collage, "The Many Faces of Cape Verde." He was pleased and thanked me. There were others waiting to see him, so I bid him good day and left. At about 09:00 I went across to my cousin Irmano Rodrigues's restaurant and had breakfast.

**11-08-07 Thursday:** Awake at 04:30, washed and did gongyo. Today I will be going to Sao Filipe again. I will try to find my cousin Emma in Largarice. Chico was up early to unlock the front door and see me off when the Lugar came at 06:00. The Lugar was about 10 minutes late. It was still dark out with a cool breeze coming off the ocean. The bus (Lugar) traveled west to Fajazinha to pickup passengers and then returning through Murro, Sumbango, on to Quimada-Guincho, Igreja, Relva, and points west along the southern route to Sao Filipe.

The sun was rising and it was another beautiful day on Fogo. There are so many beautiful scenes to see on this southern route. The volcano Pico dominates the view to the West and the hazy sea to the East is restful to the eyes. The sun rises and breaks through the haze and scattered clouds. The narrow cobblestone road winds and climbs around the many gorges formed by the ancient and recent lava flows of the Fogo volcano. The flowers, banana trees, the people on their way to work, and children on their way to school, are all the interesting things to see as I travel this route. I wish I had the time to just stay awhile in each location to take in all the sites, explore and record all the beauty that Fogo has to offer.

I arrived in Sao Filipe at about 08:15. Went down to the Sea Food Restaurant to have breakfast and wait for Leroy. At 09:22, I called Leroy. He was taking some people to the airport and will meet me shortly. While waiting, I overheard a man talking about selling his land. I suggested that he lease or rent rather than sell. So many Cape Verdeans are selling land at what they think is a good price, but the little money they get will be gone and so will the control of the land be shifted to outside developers.

09:49, I look out to the waters between Brava and Fogo and the sea is changing from smooth and calm to rough, as the current from the North moves in against the wind coming from the South. Leroy and Bo boi arrive at 10:00. We have breakfast, which consists of an egg omelet over catchupa, coffee, bread, goat cheese and a banana. Leroy had his usual egg soup and tea. After breakfast, we set out to find Largarice and my cousin Emma who we were told was at Salvador's house. When we got up to the general area of Largarice, we ask a woman for directions to Salvador's house. She kindly gave us directions and we drove up to the house. I walked up to the door and introduced myself to Salvador. He called to his wife to go and get Emma. It was a very eventful meeting.

My cousin Emma is almost completely deaf and blind. For her to hear, you have to talk loudly into her ear. She began to cry when she found out who I was. She said she had been praying many years to be able to see her American cousins. She asked about my father, my uncle Roche, and two aunts, Peggy and Anna. She was so overjoyed to finally meet her grandmother's grandchild. It was a very emotional time for me as well. Now I have completed the Cape Verdean connection for both my grandfather and grandmother. Thanks to the support of my friend Leroy

Gonsalves. I have finally reunited the American and Cape Verdean sides of the Rodrigues, Gonsalves, Pina, and Pires Families. I took pictures and video of this occasion. The visit was to brief. I hope I will get back to see her soon.

**(Fig: 28) Cousin Emma**

Today I have completed my mission of making a reconnection with both my grandfather's family and grandmother's family. A gap of 96 to 98 years of separation has been bridged. In 2005 reconnecting with my grandfather's place of birth and today, my grandmother's place of birth.

Another mission on this day was to go to where Jack Barboza was born. Jack was born in an area called Sao Lauranco. I have been told by my cousin Guenny P., that I have an uncle "Bo boi" who lives there who will help me locate Jack's family and even host my stay while there. Leroy will take me to find him today.

We traveled to a place in Sao Lauranco called "Pedrome." I met with Uncle "Bo'Boi" at his home. I asked him if I would be able to stay at his home for a few days and he said I was welcome to stay as long as I needed.

**(Fig: 29) Bo'Boi and Leroy**

I arranged to stay with him the week of November 12 to the sixteenth, as I was due to leave Cape Verde on 20 November. I was also able to find the house of Prof. Ildo B., the head of schools in the area, who could help me with information on Jack. I also was able to confirm that my uncle, Raul R. Pires, who was a childhood contemporary of Jack Barbosa, may at 98 years old have some recollection of Jack's childhood days. Raul is 8 years younger than Jack so he may not remember him. Raul at 98 has not been in the best of health lately. I hope I find him in good spirits when I meet him next week. I thank Bo boi for his help and say goodbye until next week. Leroy took me back to Chico's in Murro. On Monday, I will meet him in Sao Filipe and he will take me to Bo'Boi's house in Pedrome. I hope I can find all the information I am seeking to work on Jack's story during the four-day stay in Sao Lauranco.

Today has seen great progress: 1) I was able to connect with Guenny's Uncle Bo'Boi and arranged to stay in the Sao Lauranco area to gather information and images of Jack's birthplace to tell his story; 2) I was finally able to meet my grandmother's granddaughter, Emma and her son Salvador. Everything is falling into place. My prayers are being answered.

**11-09-07 Friday:** Today I was up at 06:30, washed, did gongyo. At 07:45, I went to have my breakfast. At 08:00, Chico went into Igreja to take care of some business. While Chico was out, Natalia explains to me about her father needing help with the household at this time. She comes from her home every morning to cook and clean. She also helps by going out and working in the cornfields, as well as tending to the cows.

She gets many sewing jobs, but she has little time to work on her business. She will be glad when Antonia comes back (Chico's spouse). Then she will have time to do her own work. She saw a new sewing machine she would like to buy for $10,000.00 CVE. Natalia has done so much for me while I have been here. Since Chico will not take any money from me while I stay here. I gave Natalia $5,000.00 CVE to help her get her new sewing machine. She was very happy and thanked me for the gift.

11:00 CV time (08:00 US time). I went up to Fajazinha to use the public phone to call Clara. The call cost $2800.00 CVE. She told me that a teacher friend of mine, Tony C. had died on November 3. It was very cold on the Cape, she said. I told her to call the fuel oil Co. to fill the tank. I told her about my meeting with my grandmother's granddaughter in Largarice. She is my aunt Mimi's daughter. She is in her 70's and lives with her son Salvador.

**11-10-07 Saturday:** Today I was up at 06:00, washed, did Gongyo. Went down to breakfast at 07:30, Natalia had prepared eggs, fresh bread and coffee. 08:45 Chico was already out. Antonia was supposed to arrive sometime today. I decided to take a walk up to Fajazinha and to the bay. I stopped by the fishing boat landing and took a few photographs. I was going to try to go on to the beach at the bay, but decided against going alone due to possible danger of falling rocks. The path to the bay is very narrow and slippery in places. I was wearing flip-flops, (not the best things to wear hiking a rocky trail), and I was not familiar with the area. I would have to wait and go with someone local.

Just a little past the fish landing I found a pleasant cool spot where I could sit and observe the beautiful view of the bay and the sea. The spot was next to a stonewall that created a shaded area with a refreshing cool breeze blowing by. I watched and listened to wave trains constantly crashing onto the beach and volcanic outcrops. Up the road toward Fajazinha there are workers building a retaining seawall and building a new roadbed coming to the fish landing area.

I walked back to the fishing boat landing took some pictures and get my feet in the water. I think the tide is coming in, as the waves are coming in closer to the landing. The sand here is black and fine; made up of volcanic granules that are gritty and sharp. Each wave carries with it a great deal of this grit and is not very kind to bare skin. The grit sticks in between my toes and surface of my flip-flops. I place my camera on a ledge, with the bay and cliffs as a backdrop take some self-portraits.

The undertow was very strong. In water up to my calves, I was almost knocked down by the waves undermining the sand under my feet, threatening to knock me down. My flip-flops became very slippery, making it difficult to walk in them. After cleaning the grit from between my toes, I made it up to a dry bench above the landing, cleaned my feet, and dried off my flip-flops.

I propped my camcorder on the fish worktable and recorded my own comments about being in the place my grandfather was born and played as a child.

Two Fishermen approach the table and start working on some kind of hand fishing device.

**(Fig: 30) Fogo Fisher**

One cuts a board into a rectangle and begins to smooth the edges. While the other sits and watches, he then ties fishing line on it and winds the line around the rectangle shaped board. The device is used to fish from the rocks or the shore. When I identify myself, I am told that we are related. I take more pictures of him and the area.

**(Fig: 31) Village of Fajazinha and Murro**

My grandfather lived and played in this area until his twenties and then left for America in 1909, never to see Cape Verde again. It feels strange that here I am, almost 100 years later, walking on the same grounds he knew as a child and young adult, looking at the same bay and mountains he looked at back then. Not a whole lot has changed since then, except many new houses have been built. All houses now have electricity; most have telephones and indoor toilets. Automobiles travel stone paved roads, which were once footpaths for people & animals. The biggest change is the fact that Cape Verde is now a free republic and no longer under the colonial rule of Portugal.

I am very proud of the fact that it was my grandfather's first cousin, the current President of Cape Verde, Pedro V. Pires who had a hand in making this freedom from Portugal possible. Under President Pires and the Prime

Minister Jose Maria Neves, after only 32 years as a Republic, Cape Verde
has moved from an underdeveloped nation to a nation that has moved into
a position of a medium developed nation that is rapidly progressing as a
first rate democratic nation.

There is a strong effort to realize the current government goals of better
education, health care, and improvement in infrastructure. I observed
many activities such as, construction of new schools, a new hospital, water
works, and retaining walls, repair of roads and house construction all over
the Island of Fogo.

There is also a need for more awareness by the people of Cape Verde that
their land is the most precious asset and that they need to maintain control
and not sell land just for immediate profit, but lease or rent to developers
as opposed to selling. Cape Verdean landowners should be encouraged in
this way. Cape Verde has tremendous potential and the nature and quality
of the Islands should be protected from uncontrolled exploitation. The
quality of life and people must also be protected from exploitive labor
practices. There should be an establishment of a minimum living wage for
all labor. Presently the labor types of jobs that exist do not provide a decent
living wage. From what I have observed, there is a great contrast between
the professional class and the nonprofessional. I have been told that many
people get paid in food, rather than cash.

Chico's spouse, Antonia is arriving today from America. It is 14:50 and
there is no word of Antonia's flight arriving. Chico called his son Nene.
Nene is still in Bila (Sao Filipe), no word of the status of her flight from
America. No word yet, of its arrival in Praia. We sit and wait. Chico sighs,
"Ah! Nho Vasco. Vasco Rodrigues Pires." (That is what my name should
have been had my father followed the Cape Verdean naming tradition of
using the paternal family middle name.) I asked Chico when did he first
go to America. "I went to America on the Schooner Ernestina in 1957,"
he told me.

That was the same year I met my other cousin, Mane G. Andrade, my
grandmother's nephew, for the first time. He was working on the Schooner
Ernestina as a cook. I guess that was when I first met Chico. Chico told me
that my grandfather, Nicholau R. Pires, who is Chico's uncle, helped him a
great deal with needed money and other assistance when he first arrived in
America. Chico said the trip across took 28 days from the city of Mendello
on the Island Of Sao Vicente, Cabo Verde to Providence, RI, USA. The
cost of the trip was $1000.00. (Not sure if he meant CVE or USD) While
in the US he found a job working in a bakery in the city of Boston, Ma. He

worked there for 11 years, until he was injured in an accident (got finger cut off) and never went back to work there again.

It is 15:30 and still there was no word on Antonia's flight from the USA. At about 15:50 Antonia arrives with Nene. The plane was late leaving Boston and arrived in Praia around noontime. Chico was very happy to see Antonia. She was also meeting her new grandson, Diogo Monteiro Garcia Pires, for the first time. Diogo is just less than a year-old. She also announced that she had finally received her American citizenship and was proudly waving her US Passport around. I wondered how long it would take me to get my CV citizenship. I put in an application back in October. Antonia was very happy to be back in her house again, after almost a year in the States.

**11-11-07 Sunday:** Up at 06:30 wash and did gongyo. At 07:30, I went down stairs for breakfast. Eggs, bread, bulasas, and coffee were served. I had planned to go to church with Antonia, but she will not be going today. After breakfast, I was invited by my cousin Alerio to stop by his house for coffee. Alerio finally remembered who I was and apologized for the slip of memory. I had a second breakfast of eggs, couscous, bulasas, and coffee with him. We talked awhile and he taught me the Kriolu words for clouds and sea, "Neovo" and "Mar."

After going back to Chico's I asked Antonia about getting some Fogo coffee to take home. She referred me to Natalia. Natalia said that if I buy a kilo of coffee beans, she would grind them and pack it so I could take it home.

At 16:00, my cousin Viriato and I went down to Qaimada-Guincho to watch the championship football match between the village of Murro and Sumbango. After two 30 minute overtime periods and because it was getting too dark to continue, the game ended in a one to one tie. I recorded the game on video and still photos.

**11-12-07 Monday:** Up at 04:30, wash and did gongyo. Today, I will be going to Sao Filipe again. The Lugar arrived at about 06:15. Again, as it usually does, the bus makes the rounds up to the village of Fajazinha, back through Murro, making a stop in the village of Sumbango, then on to the villages of Qaimada-Guincho, continuing on to Igreja and picking up passengers along the South coastal road of Fogo.

There is so much beauty here; I wish I could spend at least a day in each area along this route. Taking good photos from a moving bus is difficult to do. I could only take passing shots of the sites from the bus window. The Lugar arrives in the village of Sao Filipe around 08:30. I ask the bus driver to let me off at the Sea Food Restaurant.

I entered the restaurant and sat at a table next to a window with a view of the ocean and a black sand beach. At 09:10, I called Leroy to let him know that I have arrived.

Leroy and a friend Vincent arrived at about 09:25. Vincent is from Sweden and has lived in Cape Verde for 13 years. He is married to a Cape Verdean woman and they own a real estate and construction business. After breakfast, Leroy took me to the bank to exchange some money. The rate today was $74.00 CVEs for $1.00 USD. We leave the bank and depart to Bo'Boi's house in Pedrome.

I will be staying there for 4 days to work on Jack Barboza's story. We drop Vincent off at his big compound, a white walled area with a large house that is designed like a castle. We arrive in the area of Pedrome at about 12:30. I looked for a public phone to call home to let Clara know where I would be for the next four days. At about 12:45 we found a place with a public phone. It looked like an ordinary home, except they had a small store and bar. Outside the house was a red metal building that looked like a portable concession stand. When the proprietor opened it up, there was a phone inside. She flips a switch and I dialed home. Once the connection was made a digital screen started counting and added the cost of the call. The call cost me $900.00 CVEs for about 3 or 4 minutes of connect time. We then drove on to Guenny's uncle Bo'Boi's house about 5 minutes away.

Leroy dropped me off and I was warmly welcomed into the house and shown to my room by the housekeeper. The room was very comfortable and had a private bathroom. I was told to please feel at home. Guenny's uncle "Bo'Boi" as he was called, was not at home yet.

The house is beautiful and very well appointed, with tiled floors throughout. The front entry leads in from a beautiful gated and walled garden with planted flowers all around. Coming into the house is a stairway on the left leading down to the lower level of the house where there is an open courtyard with a kitchen and bathroom to the left, a large work area with an opening surrounded by potted flowers up on the main level of the house, to the right is a corridor leading past the main level kitchen, to the left directly over the downstairs kitchen, living rooms and the sleeping quarters are on the right. It then goes directly out to a veranda that extends the length of the house. The view is spectacular. From the veranda you can look down inside to the courtyard. Looking out to the Southwest you can see a panoramic view of the Sao Lauranco area and beyond to the Atlantic Ocean. At this time of day, I cannot make out the ocean due to a thick haze. There is a cool breeze blowing across the veranda, the air is clean and refreshing. Bo'Boi has planted a beautiful garden in the back of the house. The garden has a variety of fruits and vegetables; corn, beans, squash, tomatoes, onions, string beans; fruit such as melons, papaya, bananas, and mangos. A large growth of sugar cane grows near the house. I feel like I am in paradise.

There are birds nesting all around the eves of the veranda. They are constantly singing and fluttering about. In Murro at my cousin Chico's house, it was the constant sound of the ocean and the waves crashing on the rocky shore, here it was the birds. I hope this does not go on all day. Other than the birds and an occasional bus or car going by, it is very peaceful and quiet. I was amazed at the vista that was before me. I could not take enough pictures. I wanted to record as much of scenery as possible. From the veranda, I could see the church of Sao Lauranco. It looked like it was within walking distance and the public phone store was not far away.

I will stay here for at least four days to get as much information on Jack Barboza's family as possible and visit the house and area of Lugar Novo where he was born and grew up as a child. I also hoped to meet uncle Raul who is 98 years old and a contemporary of Jacks. Maybe he would remember something from when they were children. He is 8 years younger than Jack, so maybe not. I felt like I was in a dream to be here in Sao Lauranco where Jack was born and to be able to see for myself what Jack described to me back in 2001. I feel so fortunate.

It was 14:00 and Bo'Boi had not come home yet. I met Bo'Boi's spouse, Lia. She came out to let me know that lunch was ready. She told me that I was welcome here and to consider it like my own home. We sat down to eat a lunch of rice, mixed beans and squash with noodles. We had a delicious red wine and fresh fruit from the garden. Bo'Boi arrived around 2:30. After he had his lunch, he invited me into a sitting room and we had a relaxing conversation about his family and my meeting members of my family here in Cape Verde. He shared very personal information. We discussed some of the issues of the loss of cultural ties within many Cape Verdean families: sons and daughters who move away and raise families that no longer keep in touch with their cultural roots. I was very honored that he felt comfortable with me to share such information; it made me feel like a real part of this family. I felt that he trusted me. Our cultural roots are who we are. To lose that contact, is to lose oneself.

At around 16:00 Bo'Boi had some chores to do. I went out on the veranda to sit and just take in the view and enjoy just being here. The sun was slowly descending. I was enjoying the cool breeze blowing across the veranda and listening to the birds chirping incessantly. The Kriolu word "txi txi rote" came into my head. I recall that is what grandma called the little noisy crickets. It is so strange, how being here in Cape Verde, my mind starts thinking in Cape Verdean Kriolu and words that I had long forgotten just pop into my mind. This house is so well designed and livable, I think to myself, "If I had a house like this, I am sure Clara would not mind staying here." When the sun goes down, I will go to my room and work on continuing Jack's story from the Cape Verdean viewpoint.

Around 17:30, I saw the Island Brava emerging from the haze, but only briefly. I am hoping that when the sun goes down behind it, I may be able to see the outline of Brava more clearly. It is 17:45 and the birds are still chattering away. The sun moves slowly downward, slower here it seems, than other sunsets, I have watched in other places. To have this view of Brava is an extra benefit of being here.

Around 18:00, I finally get to meet Professor Agilio B. He stopped by the house to see me. We talked about Raul R. Pires, my 98-year-old uncle. He is doing well, and we will go and see him at his home tomorrow. I showed the professor my book, which he liked very much. I showed Bo'Boi and Agilio the DVD of Jack's one hundred year birthday party.

Around 19:00, the professor went home, as it was getting dark. Around 19:15, Lia called us to supper. Three of Lia's nieces and the housekeeper joined us. At about 19:30 all the lights went out. (The local power generator had stopped) Bo'Boi lit up a propane lamp and we continued supper. After supper I went to my room, did gongyo and went to bed. Bo'Boi and his wife stayed up and continued talking until after midnight. At night, the birds were quiet and the night was very peaceful.

**11-13-07 Tuesday:** I awoke around 06:30. Bo'Boi was already up and out watering his plants out on the front entrance patio. Lia was already out in the fields. I got up and washed, did gongyo, tested my blood sugar level (139) I felt fine, rested and felt happy to be here. I got some water and went outside to take some pictures. Bo'Boi had some errands to make in Bila, (Sao Filipe). The plan was to take care of his business in Bila, and then, at 16:00 we would meet with Professor Barros and go to visit with

Nho Raul. I hope there will be enough light in the house to videotape and interview him.

At about 08:45 we prepared to go to Bila. He gave me a banana and said we will have breakfast in Bila. Bo'Boi checked the tire pressure and checked out his car carefully. His compact SUV, a Toyota RAV4, was kept in an attached garage. He backed out very carefully and we headed out. He was a very careful driver. His feet never leaving the brake peddle, touching gently on it frequently while driving. As we left the house, a woman was standing by the side of the road waiting for the scheduled bus into Bila. We stopped and asked if she wanted a lift, as it was hot and no telling when the bus would arrive. She happily accepted the ride. Bo'Boi is a very attentive man. I have found it to be typical of the way Cape Verdeans have been raised, to be attentive and kind to others. This type of courtesy is something that is being lost with this modern urban generation.

We made our way toward Sao Filipe, passing by the church of Sao Lauranco and the soccer stadium and into the city. The trip only took about 15 minutes. It seemed like it was easy walking distance, but maybe not in this heat. As we entered the city, we pass by a large store complex called the "Super Rodrigues." It is like a combination Stop & Shop and Home Depot. I am told one of my cousins owns it. We drop off the woman who is very thankful for the ride, she wished us well, and we continue into town.

At 09:32, we stopped at the Advocate (lawyer's) office. Bo boi had to take care of some legal business. The Advocate had not arrived yet so we waited outside. At about 10:30 he arrives. While Bo boi was in the Advocate office, I sat in the hallway out of the sun. Several people came in to see the Advocate. The seats filled up quickly. I left to allow people who were doing business to sit. I went outside and sat in the shade of small trees across the street. The law office is just down the street from the Medical Center where my cousin Mario is the Director of Nurses. At about 10:50 Bo'Boi finished with his business. We head back to Pedrome. First, we stopped to get some fresh bread for breakfast. After breakfast, I worked on transferring photos to my computer.

At about 14:00, we are called to lunch; Red Grouper, rice, beans, squash and wine. After lunch, I went out and sat on the veranda. I could see Brava faintly through the haze. The birds are chattering away as usual. Bo'Boi comes out to see if I need anything. He seems to think he needs to attend to me. I tell him to pretend I am not here and to go about his normal routines. He seemed reluctant to leave me alone. He really is a very considerate man. He wanted to be sure that I was comfortable and felt at home.

I sit here on the veranda looking out over this beautiful vista of the Sao Lauranco area imagining Jack here as a child. It probably has not changed that much since his childhood years. I still cannot believe I am here. I am sure that Jack's spirit must be smiling and happy that I made it here. This just does not seem real to me.

Sometimes I feel like I am dreaming. The law of cause and effect must be at work here. When Jack Barboza died just 4 days before his one-hundredth and second birthday on October 12, 2003, I was more determined to tell his story. Thinking back to that time, I wished to travel to Cape Verde, see the place of Jack's birth, and meet my own relatives on Fogo that I have only heard about. At the time I had no idea how I could afford to make such a trip. Determination is a strong influence in making the impossible, possible.

My mind wanders back four years ago when in 2003, the year that Jack passed away, a friend, Andy A., tells me of a project he is working on to help the poor children of Cape Verde to get a complete education. He plans to go to Cape Verde in the fall of 2004 to implement the program. He needed help in producing a promotional video to show prospective donors and supporters at a kick off gala that was held in the spring of 2004. I told him that I would gladly do what I could to help. He provided me with some video footage, photos, and a script. The video was shown at a kickoff gala, which was attended by the first two presidents of the Republic of Cape Verde. The event was very successful. I was then asked if I would like to be a part of a 5-person delegation going to Cape Verde in October to establish an office and a local presence of CV Children Project in Cape Verde. This would be my first trip of four to Cape Verde.

I will never forget when I heard of Jacks passing. I called on Saturday, 11 of October, to set up a time to interview him on his one hundred and second birthday. His son told me that he had passed away on the eighth day of October. I was shocked! I had just visited him about a week before.

I recall going to Jack's house on his birthday, as I had planned before his death. This time only Jack's spirit would be there. It was raining. I thought of how important rain was to Cape Verde, and how this would be a very welcome event there. Today it was a sign of Jack's final gift to his beloved garden. I felt honored to be in that garden on that special day. I felt sad that Jack would no longer be here to tend it. As I walked out into the field, which was blooming with the fruits of Jack's labor just two months ago. Now the field was just overgrown with weeds and anticipating the spring plowing to start the new garden cycle again. A steady rain, like falling tears from the heavens, soaked the field. As I panned my camera around, I could not hold back my own tears, thinking of what this house and land meant to him these 70 and more years. He left a legacy for all Cape Verdean immigrants and others by achieving his dream of coming to America and building a better life. He came to America as a young man with nothing, and left America a gift that no amount of money can buy. It is a true treasure of the heart. His is a success story of living a full life with no regrets. Jack worked hard all his life, never doing harm to anyone. He respected everyone. I am truly humbled that he would have asked me to tell his story. I vowed that I must develop the courage to work and complete the task that Jack has charged me with.

**(Fig: 32) Jack in his garden July 2003**

At 16:00, Bo'Boi and Agilio took me to see my 98-year-old uncle Raul R. Pires. He was looking well and very alert. I was hoping he could collaborate information that Jack had told me. He is a lot younger than Jack, (about 8 years). He did not remember a whole lot about his childhood. He did not recall seeing Jack in 1986 when Jack came to Cape Verde for a visit. It was still a great interview because he was spirited and vigorous. I did get much information on video about the famines of the nineteen forties and information on the independence activities in this area during the nineteen sixties. After the interview, I returned to Bo'Boi house, happy with the information I had obtained. Raul will be 99 on the thirty of May 2008

18:17, the sun has gone down behind the island of Brava. The moon is a thin sliver of its self as it was the first time I came to Cape Verde. Its upturned crescent seemed to smile at me. Brava lies quiet, preparing for nightly sleep, with its two companions, the islets of Seco and Rombo, by its side. At about 20:00 we had supper, fish (red grouper), rice, beans, and greens. We talked for a while after supper and about 21:00 I went to bed.

**11-14-07 Wednesday:** Today I was up about 07:00 washed, did gongyo, and planned for today's visit with Padre Lawrence at the Sao Lourance Church, hoping to get some information on Jack. I have noticed that the mosquitoes are very bad here at night.

At about 09:00 I had breakfast. Lia was already out at 05:00 working in the fields (padjiga) picking beans and weeding. She came in about 08:30. Bo boi was also up early watering his plants. He still had not had his morning coffee. After I finish coffee, I will go down to the Sao Lourance Church to see if I can get information on Jack's birth records and any information the padre might know of those times.

After coffee, I walked down to the church to find Padre Lawrence. He was not in. The women working in the house said that he would be back shortly. The trees behind the church provided a cool place to sit and wait. I went and sat under the trees. It is very quiet here, no birds, just an occasional cricket, and the sound of a rooster in the distance. I could hear the voice of a teacher talking to her class in an upstairs room of the church school building.

Over in the church cemetery I noticed two men working. At about 10:30 a man came from inside the church. I asked him when he expected the padre to return. "Any time now," he replied. I hear what sounds like a Hoot owl and some occasional birds. There was a small hawk circling about looking for prey. I think to myself, "Well Jack, I am sitting here in the courtyard of the Sao Lauranco church, waiting for the priest to come. I am not sure what kind of information I can get, but we will see." 10:15 and still the padre have not arrived. I went back into the Parish house where the women were working and asked when the padre would return. They only knew he had gone and did not know when he would return.

I finally decided at about 10:45 to go down to see what the two men in the cemetery were doing. A younger man repairing head stones was assisting an older man. I commented to them, "So you are the ones who create such beautiful headstones?" He laughed and said, "Yes I am." The younger man was an apprentice learning the trade. I told them that I was waiting to see Padre Lawrence to get information on Jack Barboza. "Do you know anything about his family?" I inquired. He replied, "Do you mean Joaquino Barboza Fonseca?" I said, "Yes, do you know if he still has family around here?" He said, "Yes, Joaquino was my uncle, the brother-in-law of my father." I was amazed, I felt as though Jack was guiding me all the way. I guess I do not need the Padre now.

I left to go back to Bo'Boi house. I stopped at the public phone and called Clara. She said she tried to call last night but was not understood and could not complete the call. She reported that all bills were paid. She worked at WHOI yesterday and will be working today and tomorrow. The newly upholstered chair is due to be delivered. It is not cold in Falmouth. This call cost $2,250.00 CVE.

Bo Boi is going into Bila today, I will try to get a phone card and see if it is a less expensive way of calling home. I would try to do some more walking today, but it is very hot on the road and there is very little shade.

I went back to the house to sit on the veranda to do some artwork, read, and write for a while. While on my way back to the house, about 13:00, I met up with the two men from the cemetery as they were walking up the road. I stopped them so I could interview them on camera and take some pictures. The man was Jack's nephew (subrinhu). His mother is Jack's sister. His name is Francisco and his son's name is Deany. He told me that his mother's house is the house that Jack grew up in. The house that Jack was born in is just a little further up from there. His mother's name is Augustina, Jack's younger sister. I will go and try to see her later today.

At 16:00 I went back over to Raul's house and Raul's great granddaughter, Senita took me over to Augustina's house. In Lugar Novo, I met her niece (subrinha) Betty and her son David. Augustina was out in the fields picking peanuts (Mankarda). Betty did not know when she would be back. I took pictures of her, the house, and surrounding area. I also took a picture of David and had him take a picture of me. I took pictures of Jack's birth home, which was not occupied.

Went back over to Raul's house, to say goodbye and headed back to Agilio's house. He asked if he could download some of my photos into his computer. We then went up onto the roof of his house, where I was able to videotape a panorama of the whole area of Sao Laurenco.

It was about 17:30 in the evening and the sun was going down. What a beautiful view! I signed a copy of my book, "A Fraction of Me" for him. I had to leave soon because it was getting dark and I had to cross the fields and systems of footpaths that I was unfamiliar with, to get back to Bo Boi's house. Tonight, Lia made a special "Katchupa riku" (an extra special Katchupa) just for me. Tomorrow I planned to visit Jack's Sister.

**11-15-07 Thursday:** At 06:00 I am awake. Bo Boi and Lia were already out and working. I washed and did gongyo and made a DVD copy of Jack's birthday party to give to Bo Boi. I also gave him a copy of the Ernestina DVD and a CV slide show I had made. At 0900, we had breakfast, consisting of oatmeal, coffee, and bread. After breakfast, Leroy called to let me know that he would have to pick me up today and take me back to Murro. He had to pick up people at the airport on Friday. I wish I had another day to meet Jack's sister and interview her on video, but alas, my stay in Pedrome is over earlier than I wished. Leroy arrived, I said my goodbyes and thanked my gracious hosts Bo Boi and Lia. I left with Leroy and returned to my cousin Chico's home in Murro.

**11-16-07 Friday:** At about 06:30 I awoke to the aroma of fresh ground Fogo coffee brewing from Antonia's kitchen. I got up and washed, did gongyo. At about 07:10 went downstairs anticipating breakfast. As I descended the stairs, I heard Chico cry out in great distress. When I got downstairs, Antonia and Natalia were in Chico's room attending to him. He was sitting up on the bed, moaning and was sweating a lot and seemed to have a high temp. They were trying to give him pills. I sat down beside him to try to comfort him and help in some way. I felt so helpless. I had no idea what was going on with him other than he was in much distress. He was a diabetic and may be having a low sugar attack. I asked Antonia if she had some orange juice, as this might help. Antonia had called Chico's son Nene and the doctor who were on their way. He tried to drink the juice, but was unable to swallow. He then asked, "Vasco sta li?" (Is Vasco here?) I said, yes, I am right here. I patted his hand in assurance. He then put his hand on my knee and held it tight. "Es ta bon," (It is good) he said. At that moment he slumped. Thinking that it was just exhaustion, we let him lay back on the bed. With the help of Antonia and Natalia, we pulled him further up on the bed and I took a cool towel, in an attempt to cool and comfort him. As we laid him back on his pillow, I noticed his eyes roll back, which was not a good sign. He seemed to be resting, so I thought. I did not want to believe what was going through my mind. I tried to find his pulse or feel his neck for some sign of life; he was a very heavy man so I convinced myself that was the reason for not finding one. He seemed to be just sleeping I felt, even snoring. (I realized later, he was expiating the remaining air in his lungs) Chico passed away at about 07:20. I still could not bring myself to believe that Chico was dead. Antonia came by the bed, felt his legs, and started screaming, "Chico is dead!" The doctor and Nene arrived about 07:30.

There are no funeral directors or parlors in the village of Murro; family and friends do all arrangements. In Cape Verde, death is a reality that everyone understands. I recall when I was here in 2005, Chico showing me his casket that he had stored in a room off of the kitchen.

At about 17:30 on 16 November 2007, Chico was buried. I did diamoku (chanted Nam Myoho Renge Kyo) for him and put a diamoku card in the grave on top of the casket. Note: the funeral procession went from the house, west from Murro to Fajazinha, returning past the house and by his cornfields to Quimada-Guincho and then on to the cemetery. He was buried there about 17:30, within 10 hours after his passing.

**11-17-07 Saturday**: I got up before sunrise and went out to sit on the rock where Chico and I would often sit after our morning walks, and sometimes in the evenings. The last time we sat here was Thursday the night before he died. It was about 17:30/17:45, we talked and occasionally he would say, "Ah! Nho Vasco!" The sun is rising. It is 06:27 and I wanted to say good-bye to Chico and pray to celebrate his life as a new day dawned. It was the most beautiful sunrise I have seen during my stay here. It has usually been too hazy to see the sun very clearly as it rose. Today was indeed a special day. I did gongyo (morning prayers) as the sun continued to rise, peeking above the horizon. As I prayed, the twilight of dawn slowly gave way to the light of day. Life in Murro continues; it is a typical day in Murro. As the sun, slowly lights the day, people are getting up and going to work. The waves are still pounding the shore. Children are on their way to school. Everything seems the same, except; Chico is no longer, here greeting them and wishing them a good day. At 07:24, I finish gongyo and diamoku. The morning sky today, has never been clearer since I have been here. It has been 24 hours since Chico's passing. The first day without Chico begins.

I return to the house. Antonia, Natalia, and several women are in the room next to Chico's bedroom. Their lamenting cries fill the house. Today is another day of mourning; it will go on for another 6 days. People are starting to come in at a steady stream to pay respect to the family. The women go in and sit with Antonia and Natalia as they continue crying. With each new group, the crying (lamenting) starts anew. The men in the family will sit just outside of the room where the spouse and daughter are. As people come in, the men will stand and receive an embrace and condolences from friends. Some women will stay in the room with the spouse and daughter, while others will be doing chores in the house and serving food (breakfast) to the guests. The order of serving is extended first to those who are outside. First, all the men standing on the outside were served, then the men of the family.

At about 11:00, the President of Mosteiros stops by to pay his respects for the third time since Chico's passing. He came in unescorted and sat with the family men.

At 12:45, the men were called to have lunch. Kandja (chicken and rice soup) and bread were served to all. After the meal, a prayer was offered. We all stood at the table and as each finished another man would stand and take his place until all the men were fed.

At about 13:00 my cousin Viriato came and asked me to go over to his house to visit with his grandmother Te'Te. He invited me into the kitchen to have some food. The meal consisted of Rice, beans, and squash. I then went out to talk to Te'Te; she had not been well for some time. I sat with her awhile and took some pictures. I then asked Viriato to go with me to Fajazinha bay to see the black beach and fresh water spring that was there. I took pictures and video of the scenes and recorded images of our walk along the path to and from the bay. The path to the black beach is very narrow and dangerous due to frequent rock falls. There is no way of knowing when rock falls will happen. The path is narrow and at times, the footing is not very good, due to loose gravel.

On the way, back we observed the sand and gravel harvesters, both young and old. There were men, women, and children gathering sand from the rocky shore at the bottom of the cliffs. The sand is sold to build roads and concrete blocks. I took quite a few pictures of them. Back in Fajazinha, the surfers and swimmers were very active. There were many children playing in the crashing surf on the stony beach. I observe young surfers risking life and limb, riding the waves among huge rocks on the shore. "Amazing!" I think these kids were thrown in the water when they were born. They seem at ease in the water as they are on land. What amazes me is that there is nothing but volcanic rock all around where there should be beach sand. I see kids standing on submerged rocks as the waves wash over them. It is amazing that they are not injured on the rocks.

Back at Chico's house, people are trickling in and out. The President of Mosteiros is here for the second time today. It is 17:30, 24 hours since the burial of Chico. I do not know how many more days of this meal schedule and diet I can withstand. In the morning, it is a stand up rush breakfast of coffee, pieces of bread and couscous with bulasas (crackers). By 10:00, I am starving. At 12:30 it was a bowl of Kanja and bread, again we are standing around the table rushing to make way for other guests to eat.

At 18:30, the streetlights come on, and still, no supper is being served. (Unlike at home there is no snacking between meals.) At about 20:30 we were finally allowed to eat. As I sat down to eat, I felt a sharp object in my left eye. It may have been a small particle of volcanic sand from my walk today. My cousin Moodu tried to get it out with a napkin. He got a very tiny speck of something, but I still felt something there. It felt like a needle sticking in my eye.

**11-18-07 Sunday:** At 06:00 got up and washed and went out to Chico's stone seat to do some diamoku (prayers) in Chico's memory and wrote Nam Myoho Renge Kyo in the sand in front of Chico's seat. I still had the sharp cutting feeling in my eye. Back in the house, I had coffee, bread, and a donut. Went back upstairs to my room to do gongyo and repacked my bags in preparation for the start of my trip back home tomorrow. Then I went down stairs to join the family as the mourning of Chico continues. At 09:00, breakfast is served. At 10:20, I was introduced to my cousin Manu R. Pires. He is my grandfather's nephew and lives up the road in the Village of Sumbango, near my cousin Nene. He is also related to Robert and Roger Rodrigues (Roderick). Dje 'Dje' is his uncle also. I was also introduced to Pepe another one of grandpa's nephews, who lives in the village of Caimada. Manu is the cousin of Laurenco R. Pires who works at a university in the US. Laurenco is the father of Laurencino who lives in Brockton, and Sabrina A. who lives in Situate, Ma. I took a picture of Manu and his wife.

At about 14:00 I saw Leroy Gonsalves. He had a woman, Jackie L. a retired schoolteacher from Oakland, California with him. She will be living on Fogo for at least the next five years.

I met another cousin today Nilton Gomes, who is still a student. I gave him a copy of my book, which he began to read with great interest.

I signed it for him and gave him a copy of a Buddhist newspaper, "The World Tribune" in Portuguese. The book will help him with his English. The paper will inspire him in his life.

I had made a disk with copies of the photos I took of Chico and gave it to Nene. Nene gave the disk to Tata to take back to the US with him. I copied all the files to a flash drive and gave the 512 k drive to Nene.

My cousin Viriato came by to get me so I could say goodbye to Te'Te. She said to let her know when I get back home safe. I told her that I would call her on Wednesday, when I arrived home.

It is 19:00 and it is suppertime and Nene, Moodu, and I have rice, beans, and some beef, (very salty). Nene and Meme leave with baby Diogo. Natalia and I were left and stayed up talking with Antonia until about 21:30. Then we all went to bed. I have to get up early tomorrow to catch the Lugar to Bila (Sao Filipe). It was indeed a sad ending to my visit with Chico.

**11-19-07 Monday:** At 04:30 my alarm goes off. I snooze until 05:00, and get up, wash and did gongyo, (Buddhist prayers), test my blood sugar, it read 108. The best it has been since I have been here. Antonia and Natalia are still in bed. I know they must be very tired from all that has happened in the last few days. It is almost 06:00 and I have to leave without saying goodbye. If they are not up before I leave, I will just have to call them and say my good byes later.

At 06:00 on the nose, Augusto the lugar arrives, not too many passengers today. I put my bags inside and sit in the front seat with the driver Agusto. We make our way up to Fajazinha and do the turn and come back to continue on toward Igreja, where we pick up my friend Tony and his mother-in-law Madalena who lives in Salta, on the road to Bila (Sao Filipe). We pick up a couple of other passengers just outside of Igreja. Not too many people from Mosteiros going to Bila today. I take more pictures on the way. It is so beautiful here that I wish I had more time to spend in one area and photograph the people and the views of Fogo.

Madalena is dropped off at her house in Salta. I bid her goodbye and remembered how kind she was to Clara and I when we visited her in 2005. When we arrived in Sao Filipe, Tony got off at the school he attends; I say my goodbyes and hoping that we will see each other when I return to Cape Verde.

At about 08:35 I get off at the Seafood Restaurant, thanked the driver Agusto, and give him a a good tip for his kind assistance during my stay. I had breakfast, called Leroy to come and pick me up. He arrived at about 09:15. I was hoping to get by to see my cousin Emma in Largarice before I left and get her and her son Salvador's address and phone number. Leroy could not guarantee to get me there. He said he had a lot to do today. He had to take Bo boi to check on his shipment from the U.S. Jackie Lopes, the retired teacher from Oakland needed to check on her luggage at the airport. The bags had come in, but had already been picked up by her taxi driver and were on their way to Mosteiros. We had to chase down the taxi to get her bags on their way to where she last stayed in Mosteiros. Therefore, it was going to be a day of agreeing with whatever Leroy needed to do.

First, we go down to the port to check on Bo'Boi's Bidon (shipping barrel). He was told they are still somewhere in Praia. We then head to Mosteiros to find Jackie's bags. We arrive in Igreja and go to house of behind, where Jackie had stayed. The bags had not arrived yet. Jackie was frantic. We left there to hunt down the taxi. We headed down to the Shell station to see if we can find the taxi. We did see a taxi that Jackie thought was it, but it was not. "He's not the one I asked to pick up my bags," she said. She asked the driver if he knew the other driver. He said he did and called him on his cell phone. He responded and came straight away, to where we were. Jackie was happy to see that it was indeed the driver she asked to pickup her bags. She looked in the van and saw her bags. She was happy and relieved. Then, for some reason the driver ignored her and sped away! Jackie was now at her wits end. Therefore, we got in Leroy's car and chased the driver down. It turned out that he had to deliver another bag first. As we caught up with him, he was delivering bags to a woman that Jackie had met on the plane coming over so, they had a happy reunion. Jackie got her bags and found out where her new friend lives. We had a brief visit with her friend. We then loaded Jackie's bags into the car and went back to Bevinda's to let her know that Jackie has her bags.

We celebrated by stopping in a restaurant for a drink and then headed back to Bila. On the way back, we did a little sightseeing and picture taking. Jackie was happy to finally get her bags and I was happy to get more pictures and video of the volcanic formations of the fishing center at Ponte Das Salinas, a favorite tourist spot. Jackie's first Cape Verde crises and adventure of the lost luggage was in the history books.

We returned to Bila and started helping Jackie find an apartment to live in during her stay in Cape Verde. After looking at a few prospects, Jackie decided to rent a room at a small hotel, until she could find a suitable place to live for the long term of her 5-year stay. Because it was late in the day, and we were all hungry, we decided to celebrate with dinner at the Seafood Restaurant. Jackie was learning Creole very quickly.

After supper, we all went back to Leroy's apartment. I had to prepare for my trip back to the states in the morning. As I was repacking my bags, I mentioned to Leroy that I even carry my Buddhist Alter with me, and I showed him my small traveling Buddhist altar. At that moment, Jackie said, "Oh I have always wanted to get one of those. I know about Nam Myoho Renge Kyo. I used to do that in the eighties." "Thank you Gohonzon!" I exclaimed to myself. On my last night in Cape Verde, I had met at least one SGI member I was hoping to meet here. Maybe Jackie may meet the other member I was hoping to meet. Now Jackie has to realize her mission in Cape Verde. I gave her my copy of "Living Buddhism" to read; maybe it will encourage her to start practicing again. Leroy took Jackie back to her hotel. I finished packing my bags and turned in for the night.

**11-20-07 Tuesday:** Last day in Cape Verde: 05:30 got up, washed, dressed, and did gongyo. At 06:15, Leroy is up. He will be taking me to the airport. We got to the airport at 07:30, but nothing was open. We had two hours to kill so we went back to Bila; I was hoping that since we had time that I could meet with my cousin Louis at the Education Office where he is the director. He was not there yet. Leroy had to make a stop at the bank, and then we went to the Cape Cod Restaurant for breakfast. We had eggs, fresh bread, and coffee with milk. After breakfast, we went over to the Education office to check if Louis had come in yet. He was not in yet. I left two signed books, one for him, and one for the library. We went back to the airport at about 09:00. Flight check in was at 09:30. I checked in both bags to Praia. At 11:45, I boarded my flight and we took off from Fogo. It was supposed to be a 20-minute flight. The new TACV ATRs are bigger than the normal planes on this route. They need to use every available foot of runway to take off and land. The pilot wasted no time in getting into the air, using the full length of the runway for take off. There are plans to extend the runway at Sao Filipe to better accommodate these new planes. For now, the skills of the TACV pilots make it possible to overcome this problem. We took off straight away, heading south, then west and finally north along the West coast of Fogo and on to Praia, Santiago. In the past, the flight path was to the eastern side of Fogo. I was happy to be able to see the western side of Fogo from the air. I had a good seat #3E window, just forward of the propellers. I was able to get some good video of the view from Sao Filipe to the North side of Fogo, with a clear view of Pico. The window was not perfect, but I think the images will be OK. The flight was smooth and quick, it seemed a lot less than 20 minutes from take off to landing in Praia. At 12:15, I collected my bags. Check in for the Boston flight was supposed to be at 13:00 or 13:30. We were told it would be a lot later. We were able to leave our luggage and carts in line and went off to do other things. The security personnel said our bags would be okay in line. I went to the food court and got a hamburger and fries. The burger was on a very tasty bun with one fried egg on it, with mayonnaise and ketchup. A delicious cold bottle of Cape Verdean "Strala" beer, made it a perfect lunch.

At 13:55, we were still waiting to check-in through security. AT 14:15, the security check-in begins. At 15:00 checked bags through security OK, customs forms filled out, and waiting to check on to plane.

While waiting, I met some new cousins, Lourentino, Nelson, Connie and Gil Pires. Nelson lives in Praia. I took pictures of them. At about 16:00 I saw my friend Andy A. checking in through security. At 16:15, I went out and sat outside. A cool breeze was blowing. I thought to me, "Cape Verde now has four international airports. It has made amazing progress in its infrastructure and educational programs in the last 32 years since independence. It has good governance and is now no longer an underdeveloped country, but a proud developing nation."

At 16:30, I observed the former President of Cape Verde, Carlos Veiga leaving the airport and entering his vehicle. At about 16:40 it was time to line up for the final passport and security check and go into the duty free and boarding area. The duty free store area is where you can buy items to take home. I bought a couple bottles of Fogo wine for Clara and myself. I wanted to get some Fogo coffee, but there was none available. We go through the final security check into the secure boarding area.

At 17:27, we begin final boarding. By 17:45, we are all boarded and the plane backs out, heads for the runway and gets set to take off. "I hope the wine survives the trip," I thought to myself. Without any delay, the TACV Boeing 757 takes off. As we ascend, the pilot announces that the flight will take about 7.5 hours. In no time, we are cruising at 28,000 feet and on our way to Boston, USA. We are due to arrive at Logan airport at about 21:30 ET. Dinner was served at 19:30 Cape Verde time. We had rice, chicken, salad, fresh roll, cheese, desert, and a red wine. The couple sitting next to me extended an invite to stay at their home in Pointe de Verde, Fogo, the next time I came to Cape Verde. Unfortunately, I did not write their names down so I have forgotten who they were.

At 00:20 Cape Verde time we are approaching the US Coast. At 20:20 ET, we are served a snack. A sandwich, coffee, mango, chocolate cake and water. It appears we will arrive and land on time. We have about an hour or so to go. At 21:30 ET, on the nose, we landed at Logan, 7.5 hours after taking off from Cape Verde. Relieved to get back, I collect my baggage and head for customs. The passport checker was a Cape Verdean man from Dorchester, Ma. At 10:30 ET I pass through Customs and final security check. The wine made it without any breakage. Went out and boarded Logan Express to Braintree, then called Clara on my cell, she was waiting at the Logan Express station in Braintree. At 23:00 ET, we were on our way home. Arrived home at about 00:40 ET. The trip is over.

**11-21-07 Wednesday:** This is my first day home. Up at about 08:00 washed, Clara and I did gongyo and then went out for breakfast. Called Aunt Lucy; called my friends Salah and Ray; called John Dias; called cousins Gilbert and Guenny. At the drug store, I bought a 10-dollar international phone card and called my cousin Te'Te to let her know I had arrived home safely. I called Antonia and talked to my cousin Nene. This concludes my 2007 trip to Cape Verde, and my continued search for our roots.

**(Fig: 33) The Volcano Pico**

# Part Three: Jack Barboza

On October 12, 2001, Jack Barboza turned 100 years old. The Mashpee Senior Center arranged a birthday celebration for Jack. Jack was presented with letters of congratulations from, local, state and national government officials. October 12 is declared Jack Barboza Day in Massachusetts. He is the oldest living survivor of the New England Cranberry industry. Jack is still active in his garden, growing flowers and vegetables. Jack was born in the Cape Verde Islands and immigrated to the United States in 1923. Jack and my grandfather, Nicholau Rodrigues Pires, were very close friends. I visited Jack on several occasions up and until two weeks before he passed away four days before his one hundred and third birthday.

I visited with Jack in the spring of 2002. I arrived around ten A.M. He was watching television. He was watching the daily mass on a religious channel. When the program ended, I showed him a photo that I created with him standing on the deck of the Schooner Ernestina at sea, and a photo of him standing by a stonewall in Cape Verde with a Fogo village in the background. He was amazed and thrilled to see himself in the photos. Jack recognizes the picture of him I took back in 1996. He is amazed at how I was able to join two different photos to make one new one.

Jack was very happy to see me and talk about the old days. He was especially pleased to be able to converse in "Kriolu" with me. I asked him if he would mind if I videotaped him and asked him questions about his life. He was very pleased as he had been interviewed before, but other interviewers only wanted to know about his work on the cranberry bogs. He said that he had done all kinds of work in his life and cranberries were only one aspect of his experience in America. "Yes," he said, "you are family and I want you to tell my story. Ask me anything, and I will tell you," he said. My first question was: Why did you decide to leave Cape Verde and come to America? How did you get here?

Jack was born in the area of "Lugar Novo" on the Island of Fogo, the Republic of Cape Verde. (In 1975 Cape Verde became an independent Republic.) Jack tells me that this area of Fogo is very green with an abundant growth of fruit trees and many food plants. As a child, Jack had many fond memories. "There was plenty of water and life was good." He recalls. Jack remembers. "It was a very happy time." When he was 12 years old, he used to go out with his father to go fishing. This was a time when things were very nice and there was abundance in Sao Lauranco. Other parts of Fogo were not as fortunate. Conditions were beginning to get worse. During his late teen years, Cape Verde began to experience periods of drought and life became increasingly difficult. My grandfather who lived on the North side of Fogo left for America in 1909. By the 1920s, conditions were bad all over Fogo and many people who could afford it, left. Some people were lured to Sao Tome with promises of work, but ended up in near slavery conditions working on plantations for subsistence wages. In June of 1923, Jack was able to scrape enough money ($100) to book passage on the Schooner Vulkaria bound for America, and a better life.

Jack told me that the Master of the Vulkaria was "Badjaimi di Lana," (Benjamin da Costa.) The trip took about 28 days. The schooner was so old that due to being on a starboard tack for most of the trip, the port side of the hull was drying out and splitting due to constant exposure to the sun and developing severe leaks. The Captain turned the schooner about and headed for Bermuda. This allowed the port side to swell lessening the leaks in the hull before they could continue on to Providence.

Before landing in Providence, RI, the schooner makes a near Block Island. To off load an illegal cache of spirits (grogo) before going into the port of Providence. Upon arriving in Providence, the ship was quarantined for several days before it was cleared to enter. Jack arrives in America, and a new life begins.

According to Jack, Joaquino Barboza Brandu Fonseca, he was not here legally as the emigration restrictions of the 1920s were in full force. Joaquino was a hunted man for a while in the port of Providence. When questioned by immigration officials on a work-site looking for Joaquino, he would say that his name was Jack Barbosa. Which was true, but the officials were looking for Joaquino B. Fonseca! There was no Jack Barbosa on their list, so Jack was able stay in America to fulfill his dream of a better life. Jack worked many jobs in the state of Connecticut. He said he "dug ditches, laid pipes, and was a bricklayer, carpenter and all sorts of laborious work. " The only job I could not do was using a Jack Hammer. I was too small to handle it," he said with a laugh. While on the job, Jack injured his ankle and could no longer work. He moved up to Cape Cod and stayed a short while with my grandfather in E. Falmouth, Ma.

Jack was able to acquire some land in the town of Mashpee, on Cape Cod. The Cranberry industry was developing on Cape Cod. Jack worked many jobs. The most notable was his work building cranberry bogs. He would work clearing wetlands and building bogs all by hand. As Jack often said, "There isn't any job that I have not done." He would add, "I have worked in factories, dug ditches, landscaping, built cranberry bogs, farming, limo driver, truck driver, mason, carpentry, and many, many jobs, I can't tell you." Jack has had a long and productive life, and is at one hundred, still going strong. Jack has made sizable gardens over the years, but since recently, started growing only flowers and a few vegetables. Jack has many visitors coming to his house throughout the day. Jack is never without company.

Jack and his dog Chichi live in a three-room house, built by Jack some seventy years ago. Yes, seventy years ago! He built this house with his own hands. Jack has been a very industrious man all his life. His wife of many years, passed away in 1997. Now, only Jack and his dog Chichi live in this house.

Chichi is getting excited and lets us know that he is ready to go outside to do his business. Jack prepares to take Chichi out. Jack has some work to do in his garden as well. Jack has Chi'chi's leash setup for easy connection to the outside. Chichi is getting impatient, wanting to get outside and do his business of checking out and remarking his territory.

Jack carefully comes outside and goes to his garden to begin his day's work preparing the garden for this seasons flower crop. As he works, we continue to talk about his experiences here in America. Jack works slowly on the garden with his hoe, loosening up the soil, letting the spring air into clods of soil. This is a signal for the earthworms to start enriching the soil for the seeds to come. After a couple of hours Jack says, "That's enough for today." Chichi is happy to stay outside and play, enjoying the warmth of the sun and the spring air. Jack and I return to the house and continue our conversation about his experience on his trip across the Atlantic on the Schooner Vulkaria. Jack has many stories to tell. We will have to save them for another day.

Jack has other visitors coming, so I say goodbye and tell him I will be back for another day with him and Chichi.

(Fig: 34) Jack & Chi 'Chi

(Fig: 35) Fishing Skiff

**(Fig: 36) Fishing Skiffs**

# Part Four: ERNESTINA, the Spirit of Cabo Verde

In 1956, I was on board the Schooner ERNESTINA visiting my cousin Manuel G. Andrade, a crew member who had just arrived from the Cape Verde Islands. The ERNESTINA was docked in the India Point area of Providence Rhode Island. The I-195 and I-95 interchanges were still under construction. I was 15 years old and was thrilled to be aboard a real ocean going Schooner, especially a Schooner with a Cape Verdean Master, A. Jose Mendes, Sr.

In 2000, forty-four years later, I was invited to sail on the one hundred and six-year-old* Schooner ERNESTINA. Tom G. Educational Director for the ERNESTINA Commission called and asked whether I would like to be the Artist in Residence for five days on the ERNESTINA. Artist, were invited to sail for a week from Philadelphia along the Delaware River and into the upper Chesapeake. The culmination was to participate in the events of Tall Ships Delaware 2000 in Wilmington, Delaware on June 23 and 24.

On the thirty-seventh anniversary of my joining the United States Navy, I again pack my sea bag for a maritime adventure aboard ship. We left New Bedford, Massachusetts on Sunday, June 18, four of us, heading for Penn's Landing in Philadelphia. Our driver, Polly Z., the ERNESTINA commission program coordinator, crew member Scot and Barbara, a participating artist, squeezed into Polly's compact station wagon, four strangers on our way to make history on the historic schooner ERNESTINA.

We arrived in Philadelphia in a thundering deluge of rain. It was raining so hard that we missed the turn to Penn's Landing and found ourselves heading back over the William Penn Bridge and into New Jersey. We gave it another try. Despite the rain, lighting and flooded roadways we arrive at Penn's Landing and boarded the ERNESTINA. We stowed our gear and joined the ERNESTINA crew of twelve along with six other artist participants.

Amanda M., our captain, gave us an orientation to our new home. We received instructions in boat safety and were assigned to one of three watch teams. Sophia, the Chief Mate, assigned me to the "A" Watch. Besides regular duties our station, in an emergency was to deal directly with problems such as fire, person overboard, etc.

ERNESTINA is a one hundred and six year old* Gloucester fishing schooner Built in 1894 at the James and Tarr Shipyard in Essex Massachusetts and designated the EFFIE M. MORRISSEY. Designed by George McAllen, a former schooner skipper, He made her lines fine and sharp for extra speed, with a deep hull and extra heavy ballast for stability in severe gales. Her overall length is 156 feet. Her deck is 112 feet and at the waterline, she is 93 feet. Her draft is 13 feet, and she can spread up to 8500 square feet of sail. Her best-recorded speed under sail was 200 miles in 24 hours occasionally reaching 16 knots. In 1924, Captain Robert Bartlett bought the EFFIE M. MORRISSEY. Bartlett was the skipper for Admiral Perry when he made his famous expedition to the North Pole. In 1926, the EFFIE M. MORRISSEY began a new career in Arctic exploration. For twenty years, she took students and scientists to the frozen north charting the waters of Greenland and Alaska, also collecting oceanographic samples, Arctic plants, animals, and studying the life of the Inuit people. Captain Bartlett died in 1946. The MORRISSEY was sold to two brothers in New York, for $6000.00. The vessel was almost lost when she sank, as New York firefighters, flooded her trying to extinguish a fire on board. She was raised and towed to Connecticut. Cape Verdean Captain, Henrique Mendes, and his wife bought the boat for $7000.00** ($1000.00 more than what it cost before sunken in New York) Captain Mendes repaired and restored the dying MORRISSEY, to seaworthy condition and bestowed it new life. He christened her ERNESTINA, in honor of his daughter.

A Grand Banks Schooner is reborn, as the ERNESTINA, and becomes a packet schooner connecting Cape Verdeans to their homeland, in the Cape Verde Islands. In the spring of 1949, she began serving as a packet schooner bringing immigrants to the United States and cargo back to Cape Verde. In 1965, ERNESTINA made her last packet trip to the United States. She was the last vessel to bring immigrants to these shores entirely under sail. In 1982, Cape Verdean Americans and friends from many areas of the United States and Cape Verde raised thousands of dollars to restore ERNESTINA. The Republic of Cape Verde spent over 300,000 dollars to restore ERNESTINA and presented her to the United States people as a symbol of the friendship between the two countries.

In 1986, ERNESTINA is designated a National Historic Landmark and recognized with an award as an example of maritime historic preservation. Since 1994, ERNESTINA has embarked on a fourth career. As an official Tall Ship of the state of Massachusetts, She represents a proud maritime history and has become a floating classroom where thousands of children and their teachers have experienced the sea and its environment. In addition, young and old have learned seamanship through sail training.

## AN ARTIST LIFE ABOARD SHIP

ERNESTINA needs at least fifteen feet of water to float; we had to wait for the tide to raise enough to allow us to get underway. About two p.m. we depart from Penn's Landing, gliding past Admiral Dewey's cruiser USS OLYMPIA and the submarine USS BECUNA and out into the Delaware River. We anchored in the afternoon at the mouth of Raccoon Creek. The creek is on the New Jersey side opposite Marcus Hook. The Silhouette of the Refineries set against the setting sun created a view of astounding beauty. A view contrasting the nineteenth century technology of the ERNESTINA and twentieth century technology of industrial complexes along the river, and the many high-tech ships moving up and down the Delaware River. As the Artist-In-Residence, it was my role to set the program for this the first "Artist under Sail" on board the ERNESTINA. My presentation was simple and brief. Because this was such a unique opportunity of living and working as part of the crew, I felt that each artist should make this a voyage of observational sketching, picture taking and just taking in the experience. The Polaroid Corporation had provided cameras and a supply of film for our use on this trip. My primary tool would be my video camera. There was little time or space to get out painting equipment and spend time in a workshop watching a demonstration of painting techniques. I would consult with each artist individually as the need arose.

We were quickly incorporated into the working crew, we stood regular four-hour watches, checking the bilge, recording weather information, recording readings from engine room and galley gages as well as from radar on the hour or half-hour as required. At anchor, we checked our position regularly by compass as well as the radar to insure that we were not dragging the anchor. Every morning there were chores to do after breakfast. I can assure you that there is no cleaner environment than that of a sailing ship. While one watch cleaned the heads (toilets), the others did boat checks or washed pots and pans in the galley or scrubbed the deck. Cleaning the head was not just scrubbing the toilet bowl with disinfectant; it meant the whole room and ceiling as well. The floors were mopped in all living and working spaces. No food or drink other than water was allowed below deck except in the galley, where the cook strictly controlled it. When provisions came on board, everything was removed from boxes on the dock to keep unwanted guest off the ship. We soon ascertained another lesson about historic fishing schooners. There is no power driven machinery to alleviate the work.

Leaving Raccoon Creek, on Tuesday morning, we had to turn the windlass by manual power. It required six member crew to keep it moving. With the anchor secured to the gunwale, we got underway. Wind conditions and the narrow shipping channel forced us to motor down-river and through the C and D canal. This is the first time in its history that this schooner has transited the C and D canal.

During this leg of the trip, most of us managed to do some sketching as well as take pictures of river traffic, Fort Delaware and other items of interest. I could go out on the bowsprit and get an interesting video perspective of ERNESTINA underway. In many ways, New Castle from the water did not look much different today than it did in the nineteenth century.

We entered the Chesapeake and anchored at the mouth of the Sassafras River. Everyone on board was impressed with how much cleaner the waters of the Chesapeake are than the Delaware River. Laurie, the cook was a master of culinary delight. Fried Chicken, pasta, prime rib, fresh vegetables, and salad with sumptuous desserts for dinner. Breakfast was a variety of treats such as, blueberry turnovers, muffins, biscuits, and hot and cold cereals, along with pancakes, eggs, bacon, sausage, and juices. Sandwich makings left over from dinner, and other treats made lunch a pleasure. Even the heartiest appetite was satisfied; Fruit, coffee, and tea were always available. Meals were served on deck, except in inclement weather. After the meal, each person was responsible for washing his or her own dishes.

On Wednesday, Captain Amanda got us going early. Chores completed we weighed anchor and set sail. We raised the fore sail and then the jumbo and sailed down the Chesapeake. What a beautiful day it turned out to be. During our sail, we met the schooners LORNA and AMERICA on their way to Wilmington and Philadelphia. Many small boats circled us to get a good look at ERNESTINA. Barbara one of our artists lost her watercolor board overboard, due to a strong gust of wind. While this was hardly a grave emergency, the Captain decided it was a good chance to practice our person overboard rescues procedures. We all went to our emergency stations. While the Captain brought Ernestina about, we lowered the rescue boat.

Within five minutes of the overboard signal, we had picked up the victim, returned the well-soaked paper to the ship, and recovered the rescue boat. There was much good fun had, at the expense of the embarrassed artists.

The afternoon saw us head north to the mouth of the Bohemia River. By now, we had learned another lesson about historic fishing schooners. There are no showers, no hot or cold running water. I felt, I should stay down wind of everyone. However, I realized we were all faced with the same dilemma. The hoses used to wash down the deck provided some relief. However, anchored at the mouth of the Bohemia, another option appeared. While some went swimming along the side of the boat, I tried my hand at rowing a fishing dory. After dinner we celebrated the change from spring to summer with entertainment presented by all willing to participate, talented or not.

With a thunder storm moving in we drifted off to bed. ERNESTINA has bunks for thirty-six. They are narrow and hard but when you are tired, sleep comes easily. There is no such thing as separate bunk rooms for men and women. Everyone lives together. The two heads (bathrooms) are in the fish hold, which is the main bunk area. The bunks line the sides of the ship, double-decker style. There are no closets. Your possessions share your bunk. There is little privacy except in the head. The dictum is that if someone is dressing or changing others direct their eyes away.

Thursday morning, we get an early start. We motored up the C and D Canal. On entering the Delaware, we raised the fore sail and the jumbo. Several freighters and tugs passed us on the way north. About two p.m. we lowered our sails and moved to our docking location at the Port of Wilmington.

After hot showers at a local College, we spent an amiable evening at the Tall Ship Delaware crab feast and crew competition. Sailors from the United States, Russia, Poland, France, Holland, the Ukraine, and others, participated in amiable but spirited competition. Our crew proudly came away with the overall top prize.

Friday morning: Parade of Sail day. I woke early to see a magnificent sunrise. A sky filled with a mix of red, gold, green, brilliant blues and rich lavender reflected off the River. The Tall Ships lined up along the dock created an impressive image in the dawning light. Cleaning took on special significance this day. Company is coming!

We moved up to a position under the bowsprit of KRUZENSTERN to take on passengers. The A. J. MEERWALD tied up along side to receive passengers as well. We welcomed Ernestina Op Sail 2000 sponsor, Yankee Magazine, around 9:30 a.m. Other guest came later.

A half-hour after noontime, the Parade of Sail began. It turned out to be a beautiful day for sailing with a fine breeze. As we followed the Russian ship MIR into the Delaware, we set the sails. We first raised the mainsail, and then the foresail followed by the jumbo and the jib. We were not the largest vessel in the parade, but I am convinced there was not a prettier sight on the river. Turning back at New Castle and heading north, the end of a perfect sail came all to soon.

## EPILOGUE

My residency on the ERNESTINA was at an end. The passengers are gone, as well as the artists. I could now use the remaining time with the ERNESTINA to collect my thoughts and decide how I would express my experiences of the past week. It was a hard week, but one filled with ebullience and pleasure. I was pleased to know that I could do my part and pull my weight much like the sailors of old on the ERNESTINA. Cognizant that one of my own family members had crossed the Atlantic in this ship made this a profound experience for me. As an America born Cape Verdean it makes me proud to know that the independent Republic of Cape Verde was responsible for making it possible for me and thousands of other Americans, young and old, to enjoy and learn from the programs that the Massachusetts Ernestina Commission provides.

**(Fig: 37) Schooner Ernestina**

The memories will linger in this narrative, the sketches drawn and the hundreds of images recorded in video tape, camera and fixed in my mind. I hope that many more Cape Verdean people and all Americans will get involved in supporting and participating in the ERNESTINA and its programs. The state of Massachusetts should be proud to be the custodian of a true legacy and symbol of what America represents to people throughout the world.

Notes:

\*    As of the year 2000.
\*\*   Captain Mendes paid $1000.00 more for the vessel than the previous owners paid when it was in seaworthy condition.

References: Ernestina.org/history

# Part Five: Identity

(Fig: 38) I Know Who I Am

# I Know Who I Am, Do You?

The Cape Verdean writer Ovidio Martins was asked. "What was the greatest lesson that the [African Freedom fighter] Amilcar Cabral taught us?" Martins answered: "It is, perhaps, the passion with which he insisted on the necessity of carefully studying reality. Because to transform we must first understand . . ."

Recently, I had the profound experience of the power of "Knowing who I am." This piece is inspired by that experience.

A gentle English woman told me she was afraid of me. With surprise and dismay, I asked her why she thought this way. "You know who you are." She explained. I replied. "Well, thank you I am so glad you think so. However, tell me why would you be afraid of me, for knowing who, I am." She explained that in her culture she had to play a role and speak a certain way to be considered as upper class. "You however, do not fit the role that I understand you aught to play," she seemed to imply.

Wow! This was a very profound revelation to me. That this person born into a majority society of privilege and power would be afraid of me, a person of color without privilege or power, for the sole reason that I knew who I was.

Yes, I do know who I am. I know what I want to do and where I want to go. I do not subscribe to the color code to describe who I am. I am a human being put on Earth for a reason. Do no harm, be useful to others, and help create happiness. I may seem unique, but I am not alone. Anyone who understands the reality of their life, appreciates their cultural roots, and respects the unique qualities of others is like me.

Who am I? Where am I going? Yes, I have seen through the mind games, the historic "scams." Yes, I do know who I am. Knowledge of my history has set me free. The family names of Rodrigues, Pires and Warner trace back to the history of Africa, India, early America, Portugal and Spain, included are: slaves, coal miners, cranberry, tobacco and strawberry pickers as well as, presidents, doctors, lawyers, educators, even a senator or two, scientist and successful merchants. Yes, I know who I am. I do not give a damn what you think of me. For hundreds of years people of color have been kept in the dark. We have struggled and fought to get our freedom and identity back. Today, I can go wherever I choose to go. Most of all I can be me. With dignity and pride, I have played by the rules. Racist fools, will never again define my identity. I know who I am, do you? What you see is but a fraction of me. Take the time; take a closer look beyond my skin. Get to know the reality in me, and then you will understand how much we have in common, underneath our skins.

# Appendix

## The Republic of Cape Verde

**Location:** Western Africa, group of Islands in the Atlantic Ocean, west of Senegal

**Geography—note:** strategic location 350 miles off west coast of Senegal near major north-south sea routes; important communications station; important sea and air refueling site

**Population:** 434,857 (July 2000 estimate.)

**Amilcar L. Cabral**
**National Hero**

Born 1921, Bafata, Portuguese Guinea of Cape Verdean father Juvenal Cabral and Guinean mother Iva Pinhel Évora. Died January 20, 1973, Conakry, Guinea

Amilcar was an Agronomist and nationalist politician, founder (1956) and secretary-general of the Partido Africano da Independência da Guiné e Cabo Verde (PAIGC; African Party for the Independence of Guinea and Cape Verde). With Agostinho Neto, he was cofounder (1956) of a liberation movement in Angola. Educated in Lisbon, Cabral there helped to found (1948) the Centro deEstudos Africanos. He took his party into an open war (from 1962) for the independence of Portuguese Guinea.

In the late 1960s, he was the de facto ruler of the parts of Portuguese Guinea not occupied by army units from Portugal. In 1972, he established a Guinean People's National Assembly as a step toward independence. Cabral was assassinated outside his home in Conakry, where his party had established its headquarters. His three children from his second spouse, Cape Verdean Ana Maria Cabral, survive Cabral. His first Spouse was Portuguese, Maria Helena Rodrigues.

**(Fig: 39) Amilcar Cabral**

**(Fig: 40) The Many Faces of Cape Verde**

# Brief History of Cape Verde

Beginning in the fifteenth century, European countries started exploring ways to get to the Far East trade centers without using the overland routes. Portugal sent its ships down the African coast looking for a way to the orient and came across the Cape Verde Islands in 1456. The city of Ribeira Grande (known today as Cidade Velha) on the island of Santiago was established in 1462, from 1462 to 1496 the Italian, Antonio Da Noli founded and was Captain of the first permanent European settlement in the tropics.

Both Christopher Columbus and Vasco Da Gama visited Cape Verde during their explorations. Cape Verde became a Portuguese colony lasting more than 500 years up to the last part of the twentieth century.

The Portuguese made Cape Verde, a center for the slave trade. Slaves captured on the African continent, were sent to Cape Verde, processed, and then sent across the Atlantic to the West Indies and Brazil. Other then language, (Portuguese, Spanish, French and English) this fact explains why there is little difference between the cultures of people of African descent throughout the Americas. In the nineteenth century, at the end of the slave trade, Cape Verde became an important stop for the whaling vessels from the America. Because of the droughts, many Cape Verdeans immigrated to other countries. Some went to Europe and Africa, but the largest number came to the United States, especially to New England.

An armed struggle led by Amilcar Cabral defeated the Portuguese regime in Guinea. Cape Verde became independent on July 5, 1975. Aristides Pereira became the first President and Pedro V. Pires the first Prime Minister. The Government is responsible to the National Assembly and is elected every 5 (five) years.

The African Party for the independence of Cape Verde (PAICV) governed Cape Verde between 1975 and 1991. In 1991, the PAICV government allowed for a multiparty system. The Movement for Democracy (MPD) won the first (1991) and the second (1996) multiparty elections and the former governing party, PAICV won the third elections in 2001. Pedro V. Pires became President of the Republic by a slim majority. These elections, which were universal, direct, and with secret ballots, were noteworthy for being completely peaceful free and fair and for being the first in the 1990s wave of democratic elections in among African nations. Cape Verde is considered to have one of the most democratic systems and best human rights record among Africa nations.

Cape Verde and the United States have a special relationship. In the nineteenth century, whale oil was in great demand. Whaling ships from New England, found Cape Verde a strategic place to stop and get supplies and fresh crews for their boats. Because of so many American ships stopping in Cape Verde, a representative of the U.S. Government was sent to Cape Verde in 1818 to assist Americans. In 1843, the U.S. established the African Squadron in Cape Verde to catch ships, which were trading in slaves. The ships stayed until 1861, at the beginning the Civil War.

There are as many people whose ancestors came from Cape Verde in the United States as in Cape Verde. Cape Verdean individuals have been in America since the seventeen hundreds. They have fought in the Revolutionary war and all wars since, in defense of the freedoms we all enjoy today. The Cape Verdean has held many different jobs in the U.S., from working in government, as business owners, farmers, construction and have been especially important in fishing and cranberry industries.

The Cape Verdean-Americans keep strong ties with family in Cape Verde. They visit as much as they can and send money and goods to relatives and friends. In the past, ships would go from New Bedford, East Boston, Massachusetts, Providence, RI to Cape Verde, with clothing, household goods, toys, and medicines. Now Cape Verde Airlines transports people direct from Boston to Cape Verde within seven hours.

Cape Verde has good relations with the United States, China, Cuba, and many nations. Over the years, the U.S. and these countries have assisted Cape Verde, with money and experts to help improve agriculture, conservation, build schools, desalinize seawater, and improve health and education. The Peace Corps volunteers teach English and good health education where needed.

# SGI-USA

**Soka Gakkai:** (Japanese: "Value-Creation Society"), a lay religious group Soka-Gakkai has had a rapid growth since the 1950s and is the most successful of the new religious movements that have sprung up in the twentieth century in Japan; but in following the teachings of the Buddhist Priest Nichiren, it belongs to a tradition dating from the 13th century, based on the original teachings of the Lotus Sutra.

Makiguchi Tsunesaburo, a former elementary-school principal, founded The Association in 1930 under the name Soka-kyoiku-Gakkai ("Value-Creation Educational Society").

Makiguchi stressed the pragmatic benefit of religion and set as his goal three values: bi ("beauty"), ri ("gain"), and zen ("goodness"). The society suffered from the Japanese government's repressive policies toward religious sects during World War II and for a time was disbanded. Makiguchi died in detention during this period. His chief disciple, Josei Toda, revived the organization in 1946, renaming it Soka-Gakkai. In common with other Nichiren movements, Soka-Gakkai places great emphasis on the benefits effected, by the chanting of the phrase Namu Myoho Renge Kyo ("dedication to the Law of Cause and Effect Teaching") which is an invocation of the title of its chief scripture, the Lotus Sutra.

The Soka-Gakkai follows an intensive policy of introducing people to the practice of Buddhism. This increased its membership within a seven-year period (1951-57) from 3,000 to 765,000 families. In the late twentieth century, the group claimed a membership of more than 9,000,000. Today it has reached more than 12,000,000.

Groups associated with Soka-Gakkai International established by it's President, Daisaku Ikeda in 1975 on the US Territory of Guam, has been started in over 192 countries, including the United States, where the equivalent organization is called Soka Gakkai International of America. Soka-Gakkai International conducts educational and cultural activities for world peace and publishes a weekly newspaper and monthly magazine.

For more information: (visit *www.sgi-usa.org*)

# List of Images—Credits

1. 1. (Fig: 1) Cape Verdean Heros—Vasco R. A. Pires
2. (Fig: 2) Grandma Rose—Pires Family
3. (Fig: 3) Fogo Market Place—Vasco R. A. Pires
4. (Fig: 4) Takinha at home—Vasco R. A. Pires
5. (Fig: 5) Cape Verdean Woman—Vasco R. A. Pires
6. (Fig: 6) Fogo Man—Vasco R. A. Pires
7. (Fig: 7) Brava Girl—Vasco R. A. Pires
8. (Fig: 8) Schooner Ernestina—Vasco R. A. Pires
9. (Fig: 9) The Port of Furna, Brava—Vasco R. A. Pires
10. (Fig: 10) Children of The Sea—Vasco R. A. Pires
11. (Fig: 11) Cape Verdean Mother—Vasco R. A. Pires
12. (Fig: 12 & 13) Cape Verde We Are Here!—Clara Y. Pires and Vasco R. A. Pires
13. (Fig: 14) Land of Our Roots—Vasco R. A. Pires
14. (Fig: 15) Three Generations—Pires Family
15. (Fig: 16) Mr. Jack Barboza—Vasco R. A. Pires
16. (Fig: 17) Cidade Velha—Vasco R. A. Pires
17. (Fig: 18) Capt. Jose Lopes—Vasco R. A. Pires
18. (Fig: 19) Village of Murro—Vasco R. A. Pires
19. (Fig: 20) Traditional Stove—Vasco R. A. Pires
20. (Fig: 21) Visual Artist Nelson Rodrigues—Vasco R. A. Pires
21. (Fig: 22) View From Takinha's House—Vasco R. A. Pires
22. (Fig: 23) Takinha—Vasco R. A. Pires
23. (Fig: 24) Sal Beach—Vasco R. A. Pires
24. (Fig: 25) Cousin Chico—Vasco R. A. Pires
25. (Fig: 26) Cousin Natalia—Vasco R. A. Pires
26. (Fig: 27) Cousin Chico & Diogo—Vasco R. A. Pires
27. (Fig: 28) Cousin Emma—Vasco R. A. Pires
28. (Fig: 29) Bo'Boi and Leroy—Vasco R. A. Pires
29. (Fig: 30) Fogo Fisher—Vasco R. A. Pires
30. (Fig: 31) Villages of Fajazinha & Murro—Vasco R. A. Pires
31. (Fig: 32) Jack in his Garden, 2003—Vasco R. A. Pires
32. (Fig: 33) The Volcano, Pico—Vasco R. A. Pires
33. (Fig: 34) Jack & Chi'Chi—Vasco R. A. Pires
34. (Fig: 35 & 36) Fishing Skiff—Vasco R. A. Pires

35. (Fig: 37) Schooner Ernestina—Vasco R. A. Pires
36. (Fig: 38) I Know Who I Am—Vasco R. A. Pires
37. (Fig: 39) Amilcar Cabral—Vasco R. A. Pires (photo)
38. (Fig: 40) Many Faces of Cape Verde—Vasco R. A. Pires
39. Front Cover Image design—Vasco R. A. Pires (Includes photo portrait of the Author by Photographer Karin Hines)
40. Back Cover—Vasco R. A. Pires (Self Portrait)

# Bibliography

Pires, Vasco R. A. *A Fraction of Me: Prose and Poetry For the New Century*, AuthorHouse.com, 2003.

Goncalves, Manuel da Luz, and De Andrade, Lelia Lomba. *Pa Nu Papia Kriolu*, 2002.

Davis, Jarita. *There Should Be More Water*, University of Louisiana at Lafayette, 2004.

Almeida, Ray A. *Nos Ku Nos:* The transnational Cape Verdean community, 1995.

Silva, Benjamin. *How Do I See Me*, October issue of Farol, (1991, p. 5, 6)

Nunes Lopes, Belmira. *A Portuguese Colonial in America: Belmira Nunes Lopes, the Autobiography of a Cape Verdean-American.* Latin American Review, 1982.

Loban, Richard. *Cape Verde: Criolo Colony to Independent Nation.* Westview, 1995.

Loban, Richard and Halter, Marilyn. *Historical Dictionary of the Republic of Cape Verde.* Scarecrow, 1988.

Loban, Richard and Coli, Trudi. *Cape Verdeans in Rhode Island.* Rhode Island Historical Preservation and Heritage Commission, 1990.

Ellen, Maria M., ed. *Across the Atlantic: An Anthology of Cape Verdean Literature.* Center for the Portuguese Speaking World, U. Mass. Dartmouth, 1988.

Almeida, Raymond A. *Cape Verdeans in America: Our Story.* TCHUBA-American Committee for Cape Verde, 1978.

Cabral, Amilcar. *Return to the Source.* Africa Information Service, 1973.

Carreira, Antonio. *The People of Cape Verde Islands: Exploitation and Emigration,* Translated and edited, Christopher Fyfe. Archon Books, 1982.

Balla, Marcel Gomes. *The Other Americans,* Marcel Gomes Balla, circa., 1979.

Babbitt, Louis J. *Visions Of Wisdom*, AuthorHouse, 2002.

Sandwich Road Teaticket Mass (Cape Cod)
Slavevoyages.org
Cabo Verde Children Inc.

Breinigsville, PA USA
12 May 2010
237886BV00001B/4/P